mexico

creating
the
style

mexico

creating
the style

KARIN HOSSACK

Photographs by Lucinda Symons

MQP

Acknowledgments

Many thanks to Dylon dyes used throughout this book and to DMC for the
generous supplies of embroidery threads. To Sue Radcliffe, who made the tin border and mosaic
table top projects, thank you for your endless interest and enthusiasm; you always
make the dreams a reality.

Published by MQ Publications Ltd
254-258 Goswell Road, London EC1V 7RL

Copyright © MQ Publications Ltd 1999
Text and projects © Karin Hossack 1999

Series Editor: Ljiljana Ortolja-Baird
Project Editor: Alison Moss
Text Editor: Casey Horton
Designers: Bet Ayer and Judy Gordon
Photographer: Lucinda Symons
Steps Photographer: Ray Daffurn
Stylist: Kitty Percy

A CIP catalogue record for this book is available from the British Library

ISBN: 1 84072 104 9

Printed in Italy

1 3 5 7 9 8 6 4 2

contents

introduction

Setting a specific style for your home is not always straightforward. Many people take pieces of family furniture and antiques with them as they move from one home to the next. An eclectic look is therefore common in at least one or two rooms in the contemporary home. Hard, clean lines and empty rooms have their appeal for some, but many would find such an environment cold and uncomfortable. As you have picked up this book, you probably find a more ethnic or eclectic style of living attractive.

It would be a falsehood to say that the projects in this book are meant to reproduce the atmosphere of Mexico. Rather, what I have expressed here is the idea that it is possible to borrow certain materials, symbols, and colors from Mexico, and create from these objects to adorn the home.

In Mexico, the word *mestizo* means a person of Amer-Indian descent. The name implies a blending, or coming together, of two worlds to form a new one. This idea forms the underlying philosophy behind the projects in this book, a uniting of cultures and ideas to produce a contemporary view of Mexican-style arts and crafts.

HANDCRAFTS

The cultural blend established in Mexico since the Spanish invasion has inspired many new and beautiful approaches to the handcrafts of the people of this hot and colorful country. Talavera-style glazed pottery and tiles were introduced by the Spanish, and quickly took hold in and around the state of Puebla. It was not long before kitchens and churches alike were decorated with intricately patterned

tableware and tiles. In the most popular colors used, blue and white, yellow and green, it is easy to see the influence of Oriental and Islamic art, as well as Spanish and Italian. Unglazed pottery is still produced, but mainly for purely decorative objects. Many of these take their inspiration from the pre-Columbian pottery of the Aztecs and Mayans. Vases with mythical two-headed creatures, and candlesticks fashioned into smiling mermaids, are just some of the products often seen. Burnished black pottery is mainly made for the Day of the Dead festivities and, because of its festive purposes, is of a low-fired clay material not designed to last.

INTRODUCTION

A comparatively new modeling material that dries without the use of a kiln or oven makes it much easier to achieve results similar to the unglazed earthenware of the ancient Amer-Indians. And the addition of a decorative edging of natural dyed raffia brings a splash of colour to the wild hare serving platter (*see page 28*).

Woven materials seem to have been inspired by basketry and mat making. The Mexican plant agave was an important source of fibers and thread, and is still used today for manufacturing thread and paper. In pre-Hispanic Mexico, cotton was spun together with feathers or animal fur to give added warmth. Today, Mexican women still spin their own thread using traditional methods. Handspun yarns made from cotton or wool range from very course to very fine. The spun yarn is then dyed with natural or aniline dyes to suit the purpose for which the cloth will be used. Natural dyes are made from numerous varieties of flowers and trees, using every part of the plant, from the seed to the bark, to produce a wide range of soft, earthy hues.

Aniline dyes, introduced through trade with Europe, give a bright flamboyant range of colors to both natural and synthetic materials, and have been widely adopted by weavers and textile workers in all regions of Mexico. Cloth from the roughest burlap to the finest silks is produced in Mexico. Symbolic colors and patterns transmit messages and information from one wearer to the next.

The importing of a wide range of threads and fibers has opened up an endless range of possibilities in the design and decoration of cloth. These patterns and colors can be used to blend a unique range of linens for home use. Bright dyes, fabric paints, and tapestry threads provide the opportunity for creative work, such as the fashioning of distinctive ethnic linens for everyday use.

CELEBRATIONS

Many Mexican festivals and celebrations are Christian in origin, and some are a continuation of the old beliefs in spirits and demons. A wide range of materials is used during the preparations. Sugar, wax animals, and skulls are fashioned for Day of the Dead. Crosses woven from palm and carved wooden statues are displayed for religious days. Church altars are strung with flowers and cut papers, while statues of saints are encrusted with *milagros*, small requests for miracles. Every state has its special fair, for example the Day of the Radishes in Oaxaca, or the Copper Fair in the state of Michoacán. Feast days of patron saints are celebrated throughout the year.

In pre-Hispanic Mexico, the Aztecs are said to have fashioned effigies of gods from the paste of amaranth seeds. They were paraded through towns and then ceremoniously eaten. This custom remains today, after a fashion. Large papier mâché *gigantes* are made and paraded in the streets; in some villages in Mexico, Judas the Traitor is wired with fireworks and ritually burned. In preparation for festive celebrations, markets are stacked with wheat and rushes, and calla lilies and marigolds scent the air. These bounties of nature will be woven into wreaths and crosses and distributed among graveyards and churches, homes and public places. *Papel picado*, or paper cutting, is used as a type of signage. In villages, elaborate cut-paper banners are strung across roads, smaller cut paper signs are displayed in the windows of houses and public buildings. These bursts of color serve as temporary heraldry to the forthcoming events and merry making.

Our *mestizo* world seems comparatively short on exuberant celebration. Fortunately, we can attempt to make each day a little less common and mundane by creating more exotic items such as candles wrapped in delicate tissue cut papers and, with the aid of fast drying paints, string our shelves with files decorated with colorful flowers and doves.

COLOR

The colors of Mexico have inspired many artists and craftspeople. The blazing sun dries the pigments of the earth to rich graded hues. Humid jungles that are draped in shadow and struck through with light, hold many dazzling displays of exotic wildlife and flowers. Towering stone temples, piled into impossible structures, reflect the rays of the sun, hiding warm, richly colored murals inside their walls. From color dug straight from the earth, to vibrant shades of neon, spectacular Mexico has it all. Colors mixed and matched together in the most unlikely combinations somehow seem attractive.

Riotous rows of painted facades line the streets of towns; everyone has a statement to make, and multiple shades of color cover every surface. The butcher, the baker, the candlestick maker, all display hand-painted signs in a boisterous competition of color. Although you may choose to live within soft, pastel walls, or clean, refreshing white, adding just a touch of unexpected color to a table-setting, or draping a colorful blanket across a sofa, will immediately add warmth and vibrancy to your home. Revive old furniture with a liberal sanding down and paint in your favorite colors. Try to apply two or more colors on any one piece, using them in unusual combinations. Change your curtains to vivid colors so that the light will be tempted to join you inside your home as well as out. Celebrate with color, splash some around and enjoy the festivities. Viva Mexico!

putting it together

When you are feeling inspired by one or more of the projects, take time to choose your color palette. Have a good look around the display rooms of arts and crafts suppliers. Spend some time perusing the shelves of a hardware store, taking special note of interesting materials such as colored ropes and wires.

All of the materials used in these projects are easy to obtain. Instead of strolling down the aisles of your usual fabric store, seek out a supplier with unusual offcuts in colors that may not have a mainstream appeal. Finding something truly different and unusual can often spark the wheels of creativity. Try not to be tempted into using old pillow cases and towels for the linens projects; treat yourself to some new ones in bold and exciting colors. The quality and colors of paints change rapidly, and it is worth keeping up to date with what is available. The shelves are stacked with odorless, fast drying paints in a rainbow of colors and hues. Have small sample pots made up for you whenever possible. If they look wrong when you take them home, there are hundreds more from which to choose. Seal the top up tightly and add the sample pot to your craft cupboard. There may come a time when it is exactly the color that you need.

Always take the greatest care of your health when working with paints and tools. Particularly with mosaic work, it is very important to protect your eyes and to clear up any splintered shards carefully,

especially where pets and small children might come into contact with them. Wear gloves if you think your skin may be harmed in any way. When painting, work outside or at least in a well-ventilated room; open the windows when working and put the project outside to dry as much as possible. In a melted state, wax can be a very combustible material, so always remain alert when working with it, and never leave hot or melted wax unattended, especially near an open flame. Above all, take your time, and don't rush through your project. The care and attention you have given to it will repay you.

10 ◄

PUTTING IT TOGETHER

table top

▶ 13

W hile you are dreaming of the transformation that is about to take place in your home, why not start your project list with a homemade hot chocolate whisk? The historical references to hot chocolate in Mexico say that it was the drink of emperors. In pre-Columbian times, cocoa seeds were used as money throughout Mexico. When the Spaniards searched the Aztec emperor's palace for gold, they were infuriated to find room after room filled with cocoa beans. The Aztecs treasured gold and silver only for their beauty. Because of the value of cocoa, only the privileged could afford to drink their wealth, which is why it was considered the drink of emperors.

Copper is an abundant natural metal mined in Mexico. Many household objects are made from sheets of copper; it is used to make cooking pots and jugs, trays, plates, and vases as well as ornamental objects and toys. Traditionally, copper was hammered; this technique consisted of a circle of craftsmen pounding in turn a hot "cake" of copper with huge leaden mallets in a precise rhythm. By using copper wire and a simple coiling method an elegant fruit basket can be made in a comparatively short time. The natural earth color and elegant lines of the copper basket speak of faraway lands inhabited by resourceful people.

Table mats woven in hot neon colors look as if they have just come over the border. Use these mats on any table to change the temperature of the room, no matter what the season or menu. The weaving is accomplished by wrapping plastic lacing around a long spiral of the brightest tropical green rope. Change the colors of the lacing at random, making each mat different, so that they add to the handmade look.

The craft of pottery is practiced all over Mexico, and like all Mexican arts and crafts, varies enormously from one region to the next. Pottery bowls and jugs stamped with symbolic patterns and creatures are thought to be some of the earliest pottery from pre-Columbian times. As trade opened up with Europe and the Orient, colorful glazes were added to the decorative techniques already in use. The ancient art of pottery has been pared down to a minimum here, with air-dry modeling material for a raffia-edged serving platter.

The art of weaving is represented by a bright cloth ingeniously decorated with painted crosses, which imitate the cross-stitch of the embroiderer, and painted motifs depicting birds, flowers, and leaves.

Mexico is a country that uses all of the colors in a palette. When planning your projects, feel free to change any colors represented here to suit your living space. Experiment with unusual color combinations and enjoy the results.

TABLE TOP

cross-stitch tablecloth

Cross-stitch embroidery is a highly versatile and decorative effect that gives an interesting finish to any plain piece of cloth. For those who may not feel confident in taking up needle and thread, here is a painting project that will give the same impression as a hand-stitched cloth. Fast drying acrylic paint mixed with a fabric medium gives a finished product that is much quicker to do than the traditional method of hand embroidery.

You may set this charming pattern of birds, flower, and leaf in any design you like. A meandering border contains the overall pattern; simple blue seed beads complete the hem. The Mexican red dye of the natural linen cloth matches the pink that the well-known Mexican architect Luis Barragán used liberally in his contemporary homes and *haciendas* throughout the Mexican states.

With the odor of tortillas frying and a pot of chili on the stovetop, this tablecloth will add the finishing touch to a home-cooked Mexican meal.

The cross-stitch painting on the table cloth might fool the eye of the most discerning needle worker.
Use the templates to make up your own pattern. When you have completed the work and the paint is dry,
set the iron to a warm setting and press the back of the cloth to set the paint.

MATERIALS
◆ Medium-weave white linen to correct measurements for your table
◆ Sewing machine and equipment
◆ Iron
◆ Lightweight card
◆ Artist's scalpel
◆ Cold water dye
◆ Cold water dye fix
◆ Fine artist's paintbrush
◆ Needle and thread
◆ Acrylic craft paints – dark turquoise, light turquoise, pale blue, leaf green
◆ Fabric medium
◆ Blue seed beads
◆ Spray adhesive
◆ Tailor's chalk pencil
◆ Ruler and scissors
◆ Saucer or plastic container

1 Wash the linen in the hot cycle of the washing machine. If possible, tumble dry to allow maximum shrinkage.

2 Dye the linen, following the manufacturer's instructions and using the correct quantity of dye for the weight of fabric. Rinse thoroughly, dry, and iron.

3 Double fold the edges of the fabric all around to make a hem ⅝in/1.5cm wide. Iron in place and stitch with matching thread.

4 Roughly cut out photocopies of the bird and leaf templates at the back of the book. Spray the undersides lightly with spray adhesive and stick them onto lightweight card. Allow the glue to dry, then cut out the templates with scissors, using an artist's scalpel for the fine points. For the flower pattern, make a template of the outermost circle only. You will have to draw and paint the other sections freehand.

5 Make as many copies of the four designs as you need for your cloth. Cut them out and lay them on the cloth in a pattern. Pin the cut-outs in place.
(see picture next column)

Paint on the crosses neatly to give the appearance of stitching. Finish off the cloth with an edging of blue seed beads sewn at regular intervals.

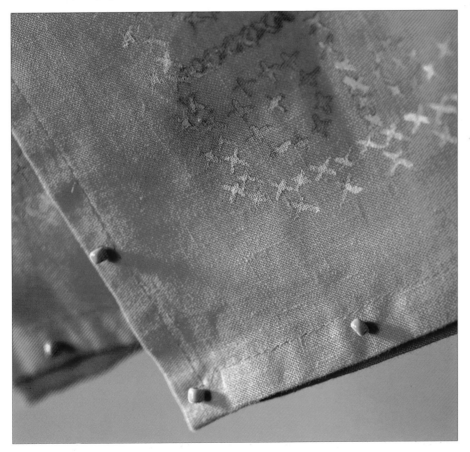

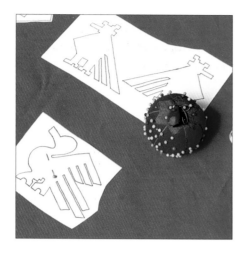

6 Take the cardboard templates for the three designs and, one at a time, use them to replace the photocopies. Holding a template in the correct position, lightly trace around it with the pencil. Repeat with each design.

7 Trace the flower pattern circle in position and draw in the center circle and the outer petals.

8 Paint in the cross-stitch, starting with the border. Pour a teaspoon of green paint into a saucer or plastic container

and add the same amount of fabric medium. Mix together. Cut a strip of cardboard 1in/2.5cm wide to use as a marker and lay it along the edge of the cloth. Alternatively, you can use the width of your ruler as a guide.

9 Paint in two rows of crosses. For the inside row, paint the crosses next to each other. On the outside row, paint them in every other space, leaving room at the corners to join the pattern up.

10 Continue painting in the crosses around the cloth. Once the two rows have dried completely, move the marker in so that the guideline is now on the inside row of crosses. Paint in the next two rows of crosses.

11 Mix the turquoise paint with fabric medium. Beginning at the corners, paint in a line from one row of green cross-stitch down to the next, connecting the two. Do the same to all the corners, making boxes on each corner. Measure the distance between the end of one line and the next. This measurement should be divisible by 3in/7.5cm. (If

not, divide your measurement into equal lengths.) Use this figure as a guide and paint equally spaced blue lines all along the border.

12 To make the swirls inside the rectangles, follow the template, and draw them in place. Paint these in with blue paint mixed with fabric medium.

13 For the bird and flower patterns, begin with the designs in the center of the cloth and work outward. Paint in cross-stitch pattern with the fine brush. Nine crosses to every 2in/5cm is the correct size for the cross pattern. If you feel unsure about painting in the cross-stitch then practice first on your photocopies.

14 When painting in the flower design use a photocopy as your guide for the petals, or draw them in roughly with the pencil. Paint in all the designs.

15 Thread a needle and sew the light blue seed beads in place along the hem. Use a running stitch and sew on one bead every 3in/7.5cm.

circular table mats

There are very few materials in Mexico that do not find themselves transformed into useful everyday objects. Weaving is one of the folk crafts practiced by women, men, and children. Some of the traditional materials used in weaving are agave fiber, palm, rush, and wheatstraw. These materials are often used in their natural colors but can also be dyed flamboyant colors to create weavings in complicated patterns.

Today people are open to the possibilities of many other materials for weaving household items. Weaving bright, neon-colored rope with plastic lacing known as gimp, creates the large serpentine table mats, which make a kaleidoscopic display. The technique used to weave these mats is taken from the practice called coiling, in which colored palm strips are wrapped around a foundation of bunched grasses in a tight coil.

Changing the lacing colors as you work can be accomplished easily by weaving the ends into the back of the mat. A trip to a well-stocked hardware store or chandlers supply store should be enough to release your imagination and persuade you to give these mats a try.

Various shades of plastic lacing and brilliant green rope are used to create a swirl of color in these practical yet decorative mats, which will add distinction to any table setting.

Spiraling lengths of neon-colored rope form the base of this colorful
woven table mat. Change the colors of the lacing as much as you like, weaving
the ends in at the back to keep them well hidden.

MATERIALS
(to make one mat)
◆ *10½ yards/9.5m lime green nylon rope*
◆ *Large-eyed upholstery needle*
◆ *Scissors*
◆ *Plastic craft lacing – lilac, blue, purple, fuchsia*
◆ *Needle*
◆ *Lime green thread*

1 Thread a sewing needle. Take one end of the rope and wrap it once around your index finger to form a small loop. Holding the end tightly in place, make several stitches to secure it. Knot the thread and cut off the end.

2 Cut a 132in/330cm length of lacing in the first color, cutting the ends at an angle. Holding one end, take the lacing inside the rope loop and secure it with several small stitches. Knot the thread and cut off the end. Now wrap the lacing all the way around the rope circle (short loops). Coil the rope around the first circle to make a second. Attach the second circle of rope to the first by wrapping the lacing around both circles (long loops).

3 The patterning begins with the third circle. As you coil the rope around the second circle, wrap the lacing around the third circle once (short loop). Next, wrap the lacing around both the third and second circles (long loop) by pushing the end of the lacing between the first and second circles. Work all the way around the circle in this way – one short loop alternating with one long one. In this way you create the spokes in the pattern.

4 Continue to work outward, keeping the spacing even. The loops will naturally

spread farther apart as the circumference enlarges. Make eight or nine rounds in this manner, leaving a 2in/5cm tail of lacing at the end. To secure the end, push it through to the back and slip it under two of the loops in the previous circle.

5 For the second color, cut a 160in/400cm length of lacing. Weave 2in/5cm of the end into two or three of the previous loops. Begin the next circle by making one long loop for every previous loop (long and short) in the first color. At the same time, make a new short loop between each of the long loops, simply by wrapping the lacing around the rope once.

6 Continue working outward with this long-short pattern, repeating long and short loops above each loop in the previous circle. Make four or five rounds in this color. Remember to weave the end of the lace into the back of the mat.
(see picture next column)

Once you get into the rhythm of weaving the rope and cord, you can create a set of mats in no time at all.

7 For the third color, cut a 160in/400cm length of lacing with a pointed end and weave the end into the last two or three loops. For this circle, make every loop a long loop, Continue in the pattern for the next two circles. For the last two circles, add a short loop between each long loop. This will help to hold the rope circles together. Weave the end in on the back of the mat as before.

8 The fourth color in the pattern is the same as the second color. Cut a length 140in/350cm long and angle the ends. The weaving that you have done to this point should be tight enough to allow you to use the long and short loops in

different combinations. You can keep making long loops only, or change the pattern by using a combination of long and short loops. Whichever way you choose to make the pattern, make two rounds, and then weave the ends into the back of the mat to finish off.

9 The fifth color is the same as the first. Cut a 160in/400cm length of this color, following the pattern in the previous two circles, or changing the pattern again. Make three or four circles, leaving enough rope for two more. Weave the end in as before.

10 The sixth color is the same as the second and fourth colors. Cut a 180in/450cm length of plastic lacing and make two circles in this color, following the pattern that has emerged. Keep the weaving tight on the last row in order to form an edging for the mat. When you reach the end of the length of rope, wrap the lacing tightly around the end and the previous row three times in close succession. Bring the tail end to the back of the mat and weave it into the previous loops. Tidy any loose ends and tighten in any weaving that may have worked itself loose.

▶ 23

copper wire
fruit basket

Natural deposits of copper are found in the state of Michoacán. Mexican metal workers make many articles from hammered sheets of copper. A traditional copper item was a pot in which pork fat was boiled or sugar caramelized for making candies. Every year during the month of August, a copper fair is held in Santa Clara. During one of these fairs 113 different groups of copper products were displayed, showing the versatility of this humble metal.

Copper wire is very soft and therefore easy to work with; bending it into loops and sewing the forms together onto a small hoop gives the structure strength. By making a small loom from a few nails and a scrap of wood, you can easily bend and fold a length of wire to form the sides of the simple bowl. To create a container out of a small reel of wire can be a very satisfying task.

After filling your wire basket with juicy limes you may have just enough energy left to squeeze out a few margaritas.

A basket of coiled and twisted wire makes a very strong structure for holding an assortment of fruit.

Copper wire is especially useful for the novice,
as it is a soft metal, easily bent. Also, the materials that are needed to make
this elegant looking fruit basket are minimal.

MATERIALS
◆ *6oz/170g 14 gauge copper wire*
◆ *2oz/60g 24 gauge copper wire*
◆ *Small round stick, 2³/8in/6cm*
in diameter
◆ *Needle nose pliers*
◆ *Wire cutters*
◆ *Wood, 5 x 18in/13 x 46cm*
◆ *Hammer*
◆ *26 headless cement nails,*
1¹/8in/3cm

1 Unroll the 14 gauge wire and cut 2
3yd/2.75m lengths. Coil one length
around the stick, wrapping it tightly.
Slide the coil off and flatten it out by
squeezing it with your fingers. When the
coil is flat, pull the loops apart until the
coil measures 23in/58cm.

The base and top edge of the basket are
linked to the sides with fine copper wire.

2 Cut a 23in/58cm length of 14 gauge copper wire and form it into a circle. Bind the two ends together, overlapping them by ½in/1cm. Secure the overlap with a short length of the 24 gauge wire, wrapping the wire tightly in order to secure the ends.

3 Cut a 46in/115cm length of 24 gauge copper wire. Hold one edge of the wire coil against the wire circle and wrap the fine wire around the loops and the circle at the same time. Work all the way around the circle, keeping the wrapping even and tight. Secure the two ends of fine wire and bind the two ends of the flat coil together, then cut off all remaining ends. This coil forms the top edge of the basket.

4 Draw two lines down the middle of the wood, spacing them 4in/10cm apart. On the top line, hammer the first nail into position ½in/1cm from the side of the wood, then mark 13 points spaced ⅛in/3cm apart, starting from the nail. Hammer a nail into each position.

5 On the bottom line, hammer the first nail in 1⅛in/3cm from the side edge and mark 12 points spaced 1½in/4cm apart from the nail. Hammer a nail into each position.

6 Wrap the second 3yd/2.75m length of 14 gauge copper wire around the first nail in the top line and the first nail in the bottom line, making a loop as you take the wire back up to the next nail in the top line. Continue in this way, looping the wire over the top and the bottom nails so that you form a zigzag shape. *(see picture next column)*

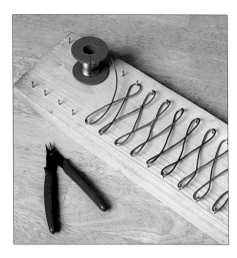

7 When you reach the end of the length of wire, carefully prize the loops off the nails and pull them apart to match the circumference of the flattened coil.

8 Cut a 46in/115cm length of 24 gauge copper wire and use it to bind the second set of looped wire to the underside of the copper circle, to which the flattened coil has been bound.

9 Bind this on in the same manner keeping the spacing even between the loops. This piece forms the sides of the basket.

10 Cut a 33in/83cm length of 14 gauge copper wire and form it into a small coil to fit the bottom of the basket.

11 Cut a 46in/118cm length of 24 gauge wire and use one end to bind the outside end of the coil to the main body of the coil.

12 Weave the fine wire in and out, wrapping it around each wire circle so that the bottom of the basket lies flat. Work into the middle of the spiral, then over and out again, weaving in and out to make eight struts. Secure all the ends.

13 Cut a 26in/65cm length of 24 gauge wire and use it to bind the bottom spiral of the basket onto the bottom of the side loops, weaving and wrapping the fine wire around both sets of wire. Keep the wrapping tight. Secure all ends and cut off any excess. Gently bend the sides of the basket to even out to the required form.

serving platter

Most ancient cultures did not have the means to glaze their pottery, just as most of us do not have access to a kiln or a potter's wheel. A hunt around an arts and crafts store can provide a solution for those who wish to create some decorative but useful pieces of pottery for the home. The air-dried modeling material used in this project comes in natural terra-cotta and in white. By using white to imitate slipware, many images can be incised or impressed on the surface of the pottery.

A hare seen in a codice in Puebla inspired the wild hare image. Codices are pictorial manuscripts made to describe the important events and rituals of life in Mesoamerica. The hare had its own day on the Aztec calendar and was a form of deity to the Aztec people.

A few potter's tools and a rolling pin will be enough to start you off on this project. The decorative raffia edging on the serving platter can be worked quickly. If you cannot crochet, thread a strand of colored raffia through the edging holes.

The colorful raffia edging adds an interesting texture to the serving platter and complements the smoothness of the "pottery."

Air-dried modeling material is extremely useful. For adults and children, it opens up the possibilities of making natural looking pottery artifacts. To help prevent your work from becoming mis-shaped, allow plenty of time for drying. To clean, wipe the platter with a damp sponge or brush with a soft brush. Do not submerge it in water.

MATERIALS
◆ *Modeling material, 18oz/485g each terra-cotta and white*
◆ *Serving platter, 12 x 9in/30 x 22.5cm*
◆ *Rolling pin*
◆ *Waxed paper*
◆ *Small knife*
◆ *Potter's needle*
◆ *Potter's modeling tool and incising tool with small pointed end*
◆ *Fork*
◆ *Paintbrush*
◆ *Size G crochet hook*
◆ *Turquoise raffia*
◆ *Large-eyed sewing needle*
◆ *Scissors*
◆ *Newspaper and cardboard*
◆ *Wet sponge*

1 Knead the terra-cotta clay to soften it and form into a brick shape. Working on old newspapers, press it down to flatten the shape a little. Roll the clay out with a rolling pin, turning it as you work, keeping to the general shape and correct measurements of the finished platter, and leaving a little extra clay around the edge. Ensure a thickness of approximately 1/8in/3mm.

2 Carefully move the clay onto the serving platter that will be your template. Adjust so that the edge of the clay overlaps the edge of the platter. Using a sharp knife, cut away the excess, keeping the knife at a 45 degree angle. Cut a piece of waxed paper the same size as the serving platter and place the clay on it.

3 Make holes all around the clay with a paintbrush handle, working the holes 1/4in/5mm in from the cut edge and 5/8in/1.5cm apart. Punch holes all the way around the perimeter of the clay. Pushing and twisting the paintbrush handle as you work will ensure that the holes go all the way through.

4 Photocopy the hare template at the back of the book and cut carefully around the outline. Cut a 3in/7.5cm square of the white clay material, soften it between your palms and flatten it onto a clean piece of newspaper. Roll out the clay to a thickness of 1/16in/2mm and a size that will fit the inside of the

The outline of the hare is scratched into the clay with a potter's incising tool.

terra-cotta platter, with a 1in/2.5cm edge all around. Place the photocopy in the center of the clay and use a sharp knife to cut an even oval shape, leaving a small margin all around the hare.

5 Paint some water on the center of the platter and, lifting the clay oval from both ends, place it carefully on top. Ease it down to prevent air bubbles forming between the two layers of material. Use your fingertips to smooth the white clay down around the edges of the oval and use the tines of a fork to press a decorative edging pattern into the white clay. Press in with the fork and pull away from the edge, dragging the white clay out. Leave the edge a little uneven.

6 Use a potter's needle to trace the hare into the white clay. Lift the photocopy off and mark in the missing lines. Wipe the surface of the white clay with a wet sponge and leave it for five minutes to absorb some of the water. Cut into the lines down to the level of the terra-cotta clay, using the potter's incising tool. Clean the tip as you work along the pattern. If the terra-cotta clay mixes with

the white clay, use a damp sponge to clean it off.

7 Wipe the entire surface with a damp sponge to smooth all incised edges and remove any excess clay from the surface. Complete the pattern by scoring the surface of the hare with the potter's needle. Leave to dry for 24 hours.

8 Remove the clay platter from the backing platter and the waxed paper from the back of the terra-cotta clay. Place the platter on a piece of cardboard and leave to dry for 24 hours, then turn it over and place it upside-down. Dry for a further 24 hours.

9 To make the edging, roll a hank of turquoise raffia into a ball about the size of a small orange. Tie the ends together as you pull them out of the hank. Using the raffia and the crochet hook, make a chain long enough to go around the circumference of the platter, plus 2in/5cm. Turn the work and single crochet (sc) once into every chain stitch. Work to the end of the chain. To make the picot edging: 1sc into 2nd ch from the hook,* 3 ch, 1 sl st into first of these 3 ch to

form the picot, 1sc into the same space, 1 sc into next sc, 2 ch, miss 2 ch, 2 sc into next sc*; repeat from * to the end.

10 Trim all the ragged pieces of raffia from the edging. Pull the edging out and flatten the work as much as possible.

11 Pull a length of raffia twice the circumference of the plate and thread it through the needle. Using an overcast stitch, sew the raffia trim to the edge of the platter, stitching through the punched holes in the rim.

12 Tie a knot in the underside of the trim and cut off any excess raffia.

TABLE TOP

hot chocolate whisk

The most popular breakfast drink among the children of Mexico is hot chocolate. To make this drink the traditional way with a frothy thick foam you need a *molinillo*, an elaborately carved and decorated piece of wood, fitted with several loose rings carved from the same branch. The milk foams and froths when the stick is rolled quickly between the palms of the hands. An up-to-date version of this magical stick can be made with coiled wires and a dowel. In place of elaborate carving, a multi-colored painted pattern is used to decorate the dowel; the wire coils are held in place with a twist of wire around the stem.

If you wish to whip up some chocolate caliente, and give your whisk a swizzle, have a go with this easy recipe:

❖❖❖❖❖❖❖❖❖❖❖❖❖❖❖❖❖❖❖❖❖❖❖❖❖❖❖❖❖❖❖❖❖❖❖❖

5oz/200g dark plain chocolate (70% cocoa is best)
1³⁄₄ pint/900ml hot milk
1 tsp cinnamon
1 tsp vanilla extract
sugar to taste

Melt the chocolate in a bowl over a saucepan of hot water. Remove from the heat. Slowly heat the milk in another saucepan, and then add to the bowl of chocolate, stirring all the time. When thoroughly blended, add the cinnamon and vanilla and transfer to the saucepan. Bring to a gentle boil. Remove from the heat and roll briskly with the whisk back and forth between the palms of your hands until bubbles form 1in/2.5cm above the liquid. Serve in warmed mugs, making sure you distribute the foam equally. Add sugar to taste.

❖❖❖❖❖❖❖❖❖❖❖❖❖❖❖❖❖❖❖❖❖❖❖❖❖❖❖❖❖❖❖❖❖❖❖❖

The coils on the wire do the same job as the loose wooden
rings on a traditional sitck, drawing air into the hot milk to produce bubbles. After use,
you will need to wash the whisks by hand. Never soak them.

MATERIALS
◆ *Wooden dowel 1-3/4in/4.5cm in
diameter, 15in/37.5cm long*
◆ *Dowel measuring 2-1/2in/6cm in
diameter*
◆ *3yd/3m 14 gauge copper or
stainless steel wire, plus three 6in/
15cm lengths*
◆ *Needle nose pliers*
◆ *Wire cutters*
◆ *Paintbrushes*
◆ *Fast drying enamel paints – teal blue,
nut brown, harbor blue, orange*
◆ *Paint thinner or brush cleaner*
◆ *4B pencil*
◆ *Medium sandpaper*

1 Cut two 36in/90cm lengths of 14
gauge copper or stainless steel wire and
one 24in/60cm length. Sand the ends
of the long length of dowel to a smooth,
rounded finish.

2 To make the spring shapes, wrap the
shorter piece of wire around the wider
piece of dowel, and the two long pieces
of wire around the narrower piece of
dowel. Wrap them tightly to make a
tightly coiled spring.

3 Slide them off the dowels and bend
each coil around to form a circle, spacing the loops evenly. Join the two ends
and slide the spring hoops over the

**A Mayan-inspired design has been used to
decorate the handles.**

dowels to ensure a tight fit. Remove once more.

4 Line the spring hoops up at one end of the long dowel. Starting with the smallest hoop, wrap it around the dowel, spacing the gaps evenly in the wire. Using a 6in/15cm length of wire, insert it inside the hoop and wrap it around the dowel. Grasp both ends with the needle nose pliers, pull them tight and twist them to secure and hold the wire spring in place. Cut off any excess wire with the wire cutter.

Attach the next two springs in the same manner, working upward toward the end of the dowel.

5 Using a soft lead pencil, and starting at the spring end, place the pencil tip close to the springs. Holding the pencil steady on the dowel, twist the dowel slowly while turning the length away to make a spiral around the length of the dowel. Keep the spacing even.

6 In a well-ventilated area, paint over the pencil line in the same way with the harbor blue, holding the brush steady and twisting the dowel. Leave to dry.

7 Draw in the "step" pattern with the pencil, making two steps by drawing three vertical lines and two horizontals, and referring to the main photograph. Draw this pattern all the way up one side of the stick between the spiraling lines. Turn the dowel over and repeat on the other side. This should give you an even spacing all the way around the dowel. Paint over the drawing with teal blue. Leave to dry.
(*see picture next column*)

8 Continue the step pattern with nut brown, painting the step line next to the teal color. Leave to dry.

9 Paint in the orange "T" shapes using a fine paintbrush, placing them into the two small square spaces between the steps. Leave to dry. Clean the brushes with paint thinner or brush cleaner.

▶ 35

furniture

T o make a truly strong statement about your decorating style, it is important to add a piece of furniture that has been made or decorated in a chosen ethnic flavor. This chapter contains four approachable furniture projects which will appeal to people of different levels of competence. The most straightforward projects, such as the blanket chest, only require painting and the application of decorative touches. Soft, majestic purple suede is used to contrast the pale blue hues of a store-bought, hand painted stool. Edged with a traditional scallop trim and copper-headed upholstery tacks, this is a straightforward means of embellishment. Change the color combinations from one stool to another and make enough seating to line a brightly painted wall. Nothing else will be needed to create a stunning, colorful display of simple utilitarian seating.

Much Mexican furniture has uncluttered clean lines, although the sheer scale of some colonial pieces can be chunky and substantial in size. An airy *hacienda* would require some very large pieces of free-standing furniture. Mexican kitchens use all manner of shelves and dressers for storing and displaying kitchenware and pots. With "unfitted" being the key word in kitchens today, the white, lime-waxed shelf could be just the piece that you are looking for. Mixed together with modern white-washed wooden units it might be left standing on a counter top and loaded with your best pottery. Alternatively, try hanging it on a wall and use it as a *nicho* to display spiritual or religious statues and emblems, or stand it on the floor for gathering odds and ends. For the worker who is inexperienced with power tools, this shelf poses few difficulties. The real problem lies in trying to decide which artifacts to display on its broad, deep shelves.

Chests came to Mexico with the Spaniards. They were used for transporting worldly possessions and goods for trade and barter. They sometimes had elaborately carved facades and covers, but they are just as useful today as

they were in the New World. Bright pink complements the silver aluminum that has been cut and glued into the panels of the self-assembled blanket chest. Many chests can be adapted to suit the same treatment. The heavy aluminum foil used in this project can be found in many craft and hobby stores.

The dark wrought iron framework of a side table is brought to life by mosaic tiles creating a flowing design of curling blue lines set against a background of terra-cotta. Mimicking a window grate design originally made of wrought iron, this pattern speaks of calm, earthbound materials. Left outdoors it should survive the elements year round; if you bring it in, be sure to protect your floors with scraps of felt or rubber stoppers stuck onto the bottoms of the legs.

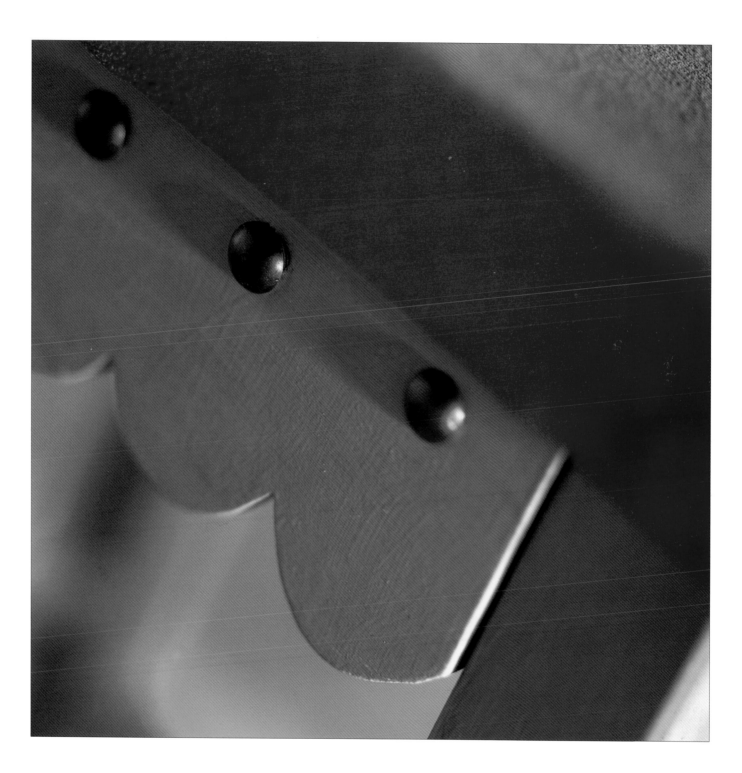

FURNITURE

lime waxed shelf

Shelves are used in Mexican kitchens for storing food and cooking utensils, or displaying pottery and decorative crafts. Shelves, or *trasteros*, range from the most rustic, rough hewn scrap lumber hammered together with a handful of nails, to the most elaborately carved or painted dressers and wardrobes.

Clean, flowing lines are the hallmark of much of the colonial furniture that is produced in Mexico, reflected here in the decorative details of the white limed shelf. The sun's rays were chosen as a theme. A jigsaw was used on softwood to cut the patterns, giving the shelf a decorative edging as well as a simple sun pattern cut into the sides. By adding height, more shelves, and a repeat pattern cut into the sides, this project could be adapted into an eye-catching bookshelf, which might display the owner's collection of Mexican art and artifacts.

Motifs inspired by natural forms are used to decorate the otherwise plain lime waxed shelves.

The compact wooden shelf can be placed on a countertop or on the floor.
The lime waxed finish protects the wood and adds a soft, natural look to the overall appearance.
Pile the shelf high with your favorite and most appealing collectibles.

MATERIALS
- ◆ *Pine boards: 2 pieces of 12 x 19 x ¾in/30 x 48 x 2cm; 2 pieces of 12 x 16 x ¾in/30 x 40 x 2cm; 1 piece of 9 x 19 x ¾in/23 x 48 x 2cm*
- ◆ *Jigsaw with medium grade blade*
- ◆ *Electric drill and drill bits*
- ◆ *15 2in/5cm wood screws*
- ◆ *2in/5cm panel pins*
- ◆ *Screwdriver*
- ◆ *Sandpaper, medium grade*
- ◆ *White liming wax*
- ◆ *Measuring tape*
- ◆ *Rubber gloves*
- ◆ *Newspaper*
- ◆ *Soft rags*
- ◆ *PVA wood glue*
- ◆ *Old paintbrush (for glue)*
- ◆ *Scissors*
- ◆ *Tracing paper*
- ◆ *Lightweight cardboard*
- ◆ *Glue stick*
- ◆ *Pencil*
- ◆ *Clean cloth*

1 On one of the 12 x 16 x ¾in/30 x 40 x 2cm boards, measure and mark pencil points at 2in/5cm, 6in/15cm, and 10in/25cm across the width, and 1in/2.5cm down from the top. Measure down 12in/30cm from the top and mark the same points – 2in/5cm, 6in/15cm, and 10in/25cm – across the width.

2 Repeat with the other board. Choose a drill bit to match the width of your wood screws and drill through all the marked points. These boards will form the sides.

3 On one of the 12 x 19 x ¾in/30cm x 48 x 2cm boards, measure and mark pencil points on the cut ends of the board at 2in/5cm, 6in/15cm, and 10in/25cm. Repeat on the second board. Drill all of the marked points to a depth of ¾in/2cm. These boards will form the shelves.

The sun motif is popular in Mexico. Use the one on page 104, or draw your own design.

4 Enlarge the sun template at the back of the book so that it measures 9in/23cm across the width and 8in/20cm high. Cut this pattern out with scissors.

5 Trace the row of leaves for the top and bottom trim decoration onto a piece of tracing paper, fold the paper in half, and trace the pattern through to the other side. This will give you the complete width of 19in/48cm for the remaining piece of pine that will be the shelf trim. Stick this pattern onto a piece of cardboard with a glue stick. Leave to dry.

6 When the glue is dry, cut out the pattern to make the top leaf trim for the shelf. Trace this pattern onto another piece of cardboard, but this time measure up from the straight edge ¾in/2cm across. Cut out to make the bottom leaf trim .

7 Working on the two side pieces, lay the sun pattern in the middle of the drilled holes, measuring 1½in/4cm in from each edge and 2in/5cm down from the top of the center hole. Trace around the pattern with a pencil. Repeat on the other board.

8 Lay the patterns for the leaf trim on the shelf boards, one along each straight edge, and trace around them with a pencil.

9 On the shelf boards, use an electric drill to drill holes into each inside point of the sun pattern, making the holes large enough to fit the blade of the jigsaw (a ¼in/7mm drill bit should fit a medium jigsaw blade). Repeat on both side boards. Use a jigsaw to cut out the sun pattern. *(see picture next column)*

10 Cut out the top and bottom leaf trim patterns with the jigsaw, then cut the board down the length between the two patterns. Next, cut into the pattern from the outside edge.

11 Use a medium grade sandpaper to sand all cut edges until smooth. Use the wood screws to screw the shelves to the sides, screwing into all six pre-drilled holes on each side board.

12 Paint the flat edge of the bottom shelf trim with PVA wood glue and attach to the underside of the shelf. Repeat with the top shelf trim and attach it to the back surface of the top shelf. Fasten with two to three panel pins to secure it in place, and then drill three holes from the underside of the top shelf up and into the trim. Screw three wood screws into these holes. Allow the glue to dry completely.

13 Apply white liming wax according to the manufacturer's instructions. Take a piece of soft rag and wipe the wax onto the surface of the wood. Cover all edges and surfaces. Allow to dry for 15 minutes and wipe it over with a clean cloth to remove any excess. Leave to dry.

MEXICO

mosaic table top

The pattern for this table top mosaic was taken from a wrought iron railing seen in Mexico City. Its design of gracefully flowing hearts and curlicues is obviously Spanish in influence. Many patterned tiles come from the area in and around Puebla, where the first advances in Spanish majolica were founded.

Mosaic is not a form of craftwork that would usually be seen in Mexico, but we can take the influences of patterning, tiling and the natural earthy colors and combine them to make a most impressive piece of mosaic work.

The wrought iron table stand adds to the rustic appearance of the table, allowing it exceptional versatility in being able to move from indoors to out, and to suit any occasion. The pattern could be enlarged to cover a large dining table or scaled down to cover a small side table. The soft earth terra-cotta color and the blue of the sky would blend into most color schemes in any modern home.

▶ 45

This table is a perfect piece of garden furniture, especially when accompanied with wrought iron chairs.

Matte-finish mosaic tiles lend themselves to the earthy colors
in this metal framed mosaic table top. Look for a secondhand ironwork table,
or ask a blacksmith to make one up to your desired dimensions.

MATERIALS
◆ *Wrought iron table stand with removable top, 9 x 24in/48cm x 60cm*
◆ *Piece of exterior quality lumber, 19 x 24in/48 x 60cm*
◆ *Mosaic tiles, 1in/2.5cm square, in 14in/36cm square sheets – 2 sheets terra-cotta, 1 sheet each of ice blue, medium blue*
◆ *PVA glue*
◆ *Waterproof grout-adhesive and grout spreader*
◆ *Terra-cotta pigment or acrylic paint*
◆ *Tracing paper, pencil and clear tape*
◆ *Paintbrush*
◆ *Protective goggles*
◆ *Tile nipper and hammer*
◆ *Palette knife*
◆ *Sponge*
◆ *Soft cloth*
◆ *Clear floor wax*
◆ *Medium grade sandpaper*
◆ *Colored chalk or soft charcoal*
◆ *Container*

1 Trace the template at the back of the book and glue it onto a piece of paper. Divide it into quarters to make four sections. Enlarge each section on a photocopier to one-quarter the dimensions of the table top. Trim the sheets and carefully stick them together with clear tape.

2 Prepare the board by sanding the surface with medium grade sandpaper to provide a key. Seal the surface with a mixture of two parts PVA glue to 1 part water, painting a thin coat over the entire surface. Leave to dry, then rub the back of the template with colored chalk or a charcoal stick. Place the template right side up on the board and tape it in place. Draw over the pattern with a pencil.

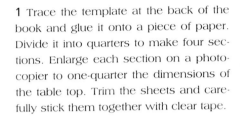

46 ◀

Fragments of blue tile form a swirling pattern.

3 Remove the blue tiles from their backing and cut them into quarters with a tile nipper. Hold the nipper close to the edge of the tile and cut so the tile splits naturally. Follow the pattern in the main photograph to make the shapes, nipping the tiles as necessary to make the shapes fit together. Lay all the tiles onto the board.

4 Place a small amount of grout-adhesive in a container. Using a palette knife, spread it across the backs of the tiles and wipe away any excess. Press the pieces firmly into place and, with the palette knife, clean away any grout-adhesive that has been pushed out around the edge of the tiles. Complete the blue pattern.

5 Wearing protective goggles, lay several terra-cotta tiles onto a piece of wood or concrete and shatter with a hammer. The tiles will shatter into a variety of small and larger pieces. Position the pieces in sections. Spread the grout-adhesive thinly across a section of the board. Press the shards

of terra-cotta tiles into this, filling in gaps as tightly as possible. Leave to dry for 24 hours.

6 Tint the grout-adhesive by adding to it small amounts of terra-cotta acrylic paint or pigment, mixing this thoroughly before adding more. Keep adding the color gradually until you are satisfied with the results. Try to keep the grout lighter than the color of the tiles, as the hue will darken when the grout dries.

7 Using a spreader, spread the grout-adhesive evenly across the surface of the mosaic, filling in cracks and holes. When the surface is covered, use the spreader to scrape off any excess. Next, with the spreader and a sponge, fill in the edges as much as possible, angling the edge with the spreader to keep it neat. If your table top does not have a recessed rim, use the colored grout-adhesive to cover the edges of the board completely, smoothing it over with a damp sponge. Save any left-over grout to finish off the table top. (*see picture next column*)

8 While the grout is still damp, wipe the surface clean with a wet sponge. Rinse the sponge with clean water and wipe the mosaic surface several times, again keeping the edges neat. Leave to dry for 24 hours.

9 If you are using a table with a recessed rim, set the board into the rim and use the left-over colored grout-adhesive to fill in the edges. Scrape away any excess and clean with a wet sponge as in step 8. Leave to dry for 24 hours. If your table top must be screwed on, screw it into place on the stand and check that the edges are smooth and covered with grout. Cover any areas of wood that are showing with a little grout-adhesive and leave to dry for 24 hours. If the edges are not particularly neat, tidy them up by sanding the grout-adhesive lightly with sandpaper.

10 Use a clean, soft cloth to wipe the mosaic surface, removing any fine grout dust. Seal with a clear floor wax. Leave to dry for 12 hours.

blanket chest

Chests and boxes made of aromatic lináloé wood are characteristic of the crafts of Olinalá in the state of Guerrero. As a result of intensive exploitation of this wood, it is now scarce. However, many alternative woods can be substituted to make chests with much the same effect.

Because chests are easily transported and serviceable for storing all matter of things, from household goods to grain and cloth, and just as useful as a bench or a settle, they were the most popular form of furniture to come out of the Spanish Colonial period.

Chests with inset panels, or "framed chests," lend themselves to decoration. Instead of a traditional floral, lacquered or painted pattern, the panels on this chest have been covered with thin craft aluminum cut in a repeat floral pattern, and embossed from the back to show detail in the petals, so enhancing the overall appearance of the panel. A bright, traditional pink behind the aluminum makes an interesting contrast with the rich red frame and shining silver panels.

48 ◀

The use of strong color contrasts, so symbolic of Mexican style, is beautifully evoked in the pink and red coloring of the blanket chest.

MEXICO

Thin aluminum can be found in good craft supply stores. You may
also find a similar material in brass and copper. Try experimenting with these to create
a unique chest to fill with blankets or toys.

MATERIALS
◆ *Self-assembly blanket chest with inset*
paperboard panels
◆ *.01mm craft aluminum, 12 x 74in*
/30 x 185cm
◆ *Fabric or wood dye*
◆ *Clear wood varnish*

◆ *Water-based wood primer*
◆ *Pink latex paint and paintbrushes*
◆ *Drill and drill bit*
◆ *Dull pencil*
◆ *Newspaper*
◆ *Tracing paper*
◆ *Craft knife and cutting mat*

◆ *Damp cloth*
◆ *Masking tape*
◆ *Contact adhesive*
◆ *Spray adhesive*
◆ *Rubber cement pick-up eraser*
◆ *2 handles with screws*
◆ *Scissors*

1 Mix the dye according to the manufacturer's instructions. Lay out the pieces of the chest and wipe with a damp cloth. Paint the frame pieces with the dye. When dry, apply another coat. Continue to apply the dye until you have the depth of color you require.

2 Lay the panels of paperboard right side up on newspapers and paint with primer. Leave to dry, then paint with two coats of pink latex, allowing the paint to dry between each application.

3 Assemble the chest according to the manufacturer's instructions. Give the frame two coats of varnish and then leave to dry.

4 Photocopy and enlarge the template at the back of the book to fit the dimensions of the front, back, and side inset panels. For a 15 x 29¼ x 13in/

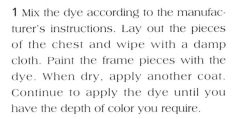

The simple markings on the petals are made by pressing the dull end of a pencil into the aluminum. This gives the metal subtle definition and creates the impression of interlocking flowers.

50 ◄

38 x 74 x 34cm chest, you will need five flowers along the center of the front and back panels, with half a flower at the top and bottom on either end. Two flowers across the top and bottom and one central flower in the middle are needed for the sides, with two halves either end. Align the photocopies and then stick them together with tape where necessary.

5 Make two tracings on separate lengths of tracing paper for each side of the chest, and one each for the front and back. Measure the lengths of aluminum needed for each panel, cutting them to fit with scissors and leaving a small margin on the sides. Measure each of the panels individually; their dimensions can vary slightly.

6 Spray the backs of the traced patterns with adhesive and lay them across the aluminum, pressing the tracing paper to smooth out any air bubbles.

7 Use a craft knife and cutting mat to cut out the negative shapes in the pattern. *(see picture next column)*

8 Lay the first piece of aluminum tracing-paper-side down on a thick pile of old newspaper. Draw in the petal outlines with the pencil ¼in/5mm from the cut edge of each petal, pressing down firmly to make an even impression. Repeat for each of the panels.

9 Check that the aluminum panels fit each of the pink panels on the chest. Trim the edges where necessary and mark the tracing paper to indicate which panel belongs to which side, and which is the top edge. Hold each of the panels in turn in place on the chest and then trace around the

pattern lightly with a pencil. Remove the panels.

10 Lay the first aluminum panel wrong side uppermost on a piece of old newspaper and, following the manufacturer's instructions, coat it with a layer of contact adhesive. Apply the adhesive to the corresponding panel of the chest, following the pattern you have traced on the inside, where the aluminum will be attached. Leave to dry.

11 Press the aluminum into place on the chest, applying light pressure with your fingertips to ensure full contact around the edges and in the flower centers. Leave to set then remove the tracing papers.

12 Repeat steps 10–11 on the remaining sides. Leave to set for up to 24 hours. Use a rubber cement pick-up to remove any adhesive that has escaped from beneath the aluminum. On the sides of the chest, at the top strut, measure and mark placement holes where the handles will be attached. Drill through at these markings and then attach a handle to either end.

suede-
covered
stool

Chairs and stools with seats made of woven palm, rubber, and plastic strips are common in Mexico. They can be bought in the marketplace or at stands by the roadside, made by woodworkers using manually powered lathes, which turn out spindles for legs and struts.

The plain stool in this project has been given a distinctly folk art appeal by wrapping the seat in purple suede and adding to the underskirt a scalloped edge, which has been painted a lighter blue than that of the legs and struts.

Furniture is one of the areas in Mexican craftsmanship where the Spanish influence is apparent. Scallop designs are a popular motif for edging on many different types of furniture. The scallop shell was once a prized object to the Spanish, showing that the owner had traveled to the church of Santiago de Compostela, where St James, the patron saint of horses and of soldiers, is believed to be buried.

▶ 53

Copper tacks emphasize the scalloped edging.

An ordinary stool can be transformed with a few items from the hardware store.
Copper upholstery tacks give a finished look to the scalloped edging that is so typical of Mexican furniture.
The top of the stool shown here measures 12¾ x 12¾in/32 x 32cm; the height is 18in/46cm.

BASIC KNOWLEDGE OF POWER
TOOLS REQUIRED

MATERIALS
◆ *Wooden stool*
◆ *Plywood, 9 x 10 x ¼in/22.5 x 25cm x 5mm*
◆ *Suede, 16in/40cm square*
◆ *Matte latex paint – French blue, corn-flower blue and paintbrushes*
◆ *Water-based wood primer*
◆ *Jigsaw with medium blade*
◆ *Sandpaper, medium grade*
◆ *36 copper upholstery tacks*
◆ *Staple gun and staples, ⅜in/10mm*
◆ *Hammer and scissors*
◆ *PVA glue and glue stick*
◆ *Lightweight cardboard*
◆ *Masking tape and pencil*
◆ *Acrylic matte medium*
◆ *Spray-on suede protector*
◆ *Newspaper*

1 Paint the stool with a coat of wood primer. Leave to dry.

2 Enlarge the template at the back of the book for the scalloped edge on a photocopier and cut out with scissors. Glue the template onto lightweight cardboard and cut out.

3 Lay the pattern down on the plywood and, using a pencil, trace it off four times. Use a jigsaw with a medium grade blade and carefully cut out the four scalloped trims. Sand all cut edges with sandpaper until smooth.
(see picture next column)

Hammer the upholstery tacks in a row below the suede rim of the seat. Use the scalloped edge to get an even positioning.

4 Lay the scalloped trim on an old sheet of newspaper and paint the top side and edges with wood primer. Leave to dry. Give the trim two coats of cornflower blue paint, allowing each coat to dry thoroughly between applications.

54 ◀

5 Sand the surface lightly to give it a slightly distressed look. Then apply two coats of paint to the legs and rungs of the stool. Leave to dry.

6 Brush a thin layer of PVA glue onto the backs of each piece of trim. Leave to dry until the glue is just tacky. Stick them in place on the frame, just under the top of the stool. Press the scalloped edges firmly into place and allow the glue to dry overnight.

7 Hammer an upholstery tack into the center of each scallop, ¾in/2cm below the underside of the seat, and one on the outer edge of each leg at the height of the lower rungs.

8 Wrap the suede around the top of the seat to check the fit. Trim any excess with scissors. Place the stool upside-down in the center of the suede and wrap one edge around the lip of the stool.

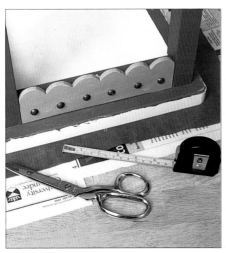

9 Staple into place on the underside. On the opposite side, pull the suede firmly until it is taut. Trim any excess and staple into place as before. Make a diagonal fold on the four corners of the two remaining sides, snipping off any excess. Staple these two edges in place. If necessary, use an upholstery tack on each corner for extra hold.

▶ 55

10 Spray the suede with suede protector. Do this outside, and leave to dry.

▶ 57

Take stock of your everyday household objects – by giving them a distinctly Mexican folk art appeal you will shift the focus of your living environment from plain and utilitarian, to multi-faceted and lively. Walls and floors take on color and pattern with the addition of a stenciled natural jute rug or a cut, pierced tin border, which might encircle a whole room, or simply run along one uncluttered, bi-colored wall. Tin is used for making many playful and decorative objects. Given a new use as a border, it will serve to brighten the drabbest wall, making framed pictures a thing of the past.

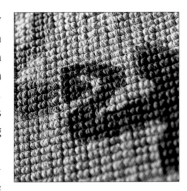

To personalize ready-made terra-cotta pots, add spirited patterns. The technique is known as *maque*. Here it is given an up-to-date look using fashionable matte colors and distemper paint to show off monkeys in wild caricature on squat terra-cotta pots. Fill the finished pots with the prickliest cactus you can find and put them where they can enjoy the sunshine.

We are all aware of the need to re-cycle if our planet is to survive and support future generations, and none do it better than the Mexicans, who have recycling down to a fine art, re-using materials that stretch the imagination and amaze and delight adults and children. Not only are materials put to utilitarian use in their regeneration, but tin cans are often used to make colorful kinetic toys and mobiles for children. The recycled tin project in this chapter makes use of large catering-size oil cans and drink cans to create a showy container for a house plant. A rivet gun and some tin snippers are all that are needed to make a display of these colorful pots. They are covered with marigold flower motifs. The marigold is a reccuring theme throughout Mexican arts and crafts, and is also a popular image during Day of the Dead festivities.

By borrowing patterns and colors from the decorative art of cut paper, you can quickly revive old file boxes

with a lick of gesso and a pot of quick-drying enamel. Use the template at the back of the book to create a ribbon of inter-linking doves and hearts with which to pattern wood or cardboard file boxes. Stacked along bookshelves, these images will add a decorative air to what can be a dull and boring filing system.

The cut paper candles look beautiful anywhere. Buy some large church candles to show off this distinctly Mexican papercraft. Use a single one as a table centerpiece, or make a number of them to cover a shelf or table top for a festive occasion. As they burn down, the thin tissue paper gently melts away with the heat of the melted wax. Any number of patterns could be created for this project, and with the array of colored tissue paper that is available, the possibilities are endless.

ACCESSORIES

MEXICO

cactus pots

Scratching patterns into layers of paint to decorate kitchenware is a method used in Mexico since pre-Hispanic days. The technique, known as *maque*, was originally worked into the surface of bowls or trays that had been lacquered with an oil or natural wax taken from an insect and mixed with natural pigments. We no longer need to make our paints by crushing insects, and if we shop around it is quite easy to find a wide variety of natural paints that will do the job just as well.

These hand-modeled terra-cotta pots have a smooth, flat surface making them ideal for decoration. The motifs used are mischievous monkey characters found on clay stamps from Chiapas. The clay stamps are thought to have been used for decorating the surface of pottery before the arrival of glazes. They were pressed into the surface of damp clay on vessels and platters in repeat patterns. The monkey is a symbolic character used in ritual dances, in which men are changed into this animal.

In these simple cactus pots the *maque* method is united with the traditional image to create a vessel for the spiky queen of the desert.

▶ 61

The monkey designs spring to life as they are scratched through a layer of paint with a potter's needle onto the terra-cotta underneath.

Good garden outlets and nurseries are always
well stocked with terra-cotta pots. Look out for the unusual shapes
with broad surfaces.

MATERIALS
◆ *Terra-cotta pots*
◆ *Distemper paints – green, gold,*
orange, lilac, pink
◆ *Paintbrushes*
◆ *Potter's needle or awl*
◆ *Clear lacquer spray*

1 Scrub the pots in soap and water to remove any surface dirt and dust. Allow to dry completely.

2 Apply the first paint color – the color you will inscribe – in the center of one side of the pot. If you are using square pots, then leave a border of terra-cotta 1/4in/5mm wide around the edges. Leave to dry for one hour.

3 Using a potter's needle or an awl, and following the designs on the templates

at the back of the book, lightly scratch the design into the surface of the paint. If you make a mistake at this point you can paint over it.

4 When you are satisfied with the design, begin to go over the lines with slightly more pressure, removing the paint a bit at a time, until you get down to the terra-cotta surface. Widen the lines where necessary, scratching away any residual paint.

5 Paint the second color on the remaining sides of the pot and around the terra-cotta border of the design. Brush paint over the rim of the pot as well. If necessary, apply a second coat when the first has dried. Leave to dry thoroughly.
(see picture next column)

6 Using clear lacquer spray, and working either outside or in a well-ventilated area, lightly spray around the outside and the inside of the pot. Leave to dry.

file folders

Cut papers are used in Mexico for celebrations in homes and public places. Village streets are draped with multi-colored cut paper banners and flags on fiesta days or for special local events. Home altars and market stalls bear the symbols of birds, flowers, spirits, and skeletons cut from variegated tissue paper and sheets of colored plastic, just for the sheer love that the Mexicans have for decoration and for display.

Both company and home offices have a tendency to become drab, monochromatic spaces where we spend much of our time. Enliven your office with color and pattern using this cut paper inspired project with dove and flower motifs to cover ordinary file folders. Alternatively, use the same technique to decorate notebooks and other flat surfaces.

▶ 63

Painted in orange, lavender, red, and green, a row of these file folders along a shelf will make pretty storage items for hiding away all sorts of odds and ends.

Cut paper motifs add a decorative touch to ordinary file boxes,
and are made more interesting when a different color is used for each box.
You may want to create some designs of your own.

MATERIALS
- ◆ *Wooden file boxes*
- ◆ *Plasti-Kote-Odds'n'Ends enamel paints – orange, lavender, red, green*
- ◆ *White gesso*
- ◆ *Small decorator's paintbrush*
- ◆ *Fine artist's brushes*
- ◆ *Paint thinner or brush cleaner*
- ◆ *Newspaper*
- ◆ *Tracing paper and masking tape*
- ◆ *Scissors*
- ◆ *Medium grade sandpaper*
- ◆ *4B pencil and rubber*

1 Enlarge the template at the back of the book, place a piece of tracing paper over it and draw around the outlines of the design using a soft pencil.

2 Sand any rough edges on the boxes, particularly around the finger holes, and

Reverse the dove design to break up the line.

wipe clean. With a small brush, carefully paint the outside surfaces with gesso. Leave to dry.

3 Take one traced pattern and cut it down, leaving a 1in/2.5cm border all around the edge. Align it on the front of the first box, pencil-side down. At the top, fold the tracing paper over and push it inside the file box to hold it in place.

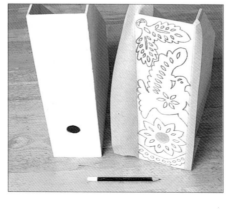

4 Tape the tracing paper in place on three sides with small pieces of masking tape.

5 To transfer the pattern, draw over the tracing with the pencil, pressing down to make a heavy line. Remove the tracing paper and go over the lines on the box lightly so they are easier to see.

6 Turn the tracing paper over and attach it to the next file box in the same way. Repeat step 5. This will reverse the pattern. Continue to work in this way for the other boxes, using a fresh tracing as necessary.

7 Using fine artist's brushes, carefully paint in the pattern, applying a different color to each box.

8 Leave the boxes to dry thoroughly. If any pencil lines remain, use a rubber to remove them.

tin plant pots

From the simple *huarache* sandal with its sole made of abandoned car tires, to water jugs and drinking vessels made from recycled glass, in Mexico materials given a new life are everywhere. Colorful tin cans are often used for making toys and containers.

For this project, a large cooking oil can is given a lick of paint and revived as a plant holder, encrusted with a flamboyant homemade version of the well-known *cempazúchil*, the marigold flower, which is seen all over Mexico in Day of the Dead festivities.

The printing and coloration on drink cans lend themselves to the multi-colored petals of this popular flower, and although they appear complicated it does not take long to produce a field of gorgeously colored marigolds, each bearing an individual pattern and variation just as nature intended.

Filled to the brim with spiky or succulent exotic cactus plants, these pots could be moved outside or in, depending on the time of year, bringing with them a welcome blaze of color.

▶ 67

The rim of the oil can is decorated with colored rope that is tied in position with twine.

The flowers are made up of layers of soda can circles cut into petals and secured with a rivet.

To obtain a supply of large oil cans, befriend a chef at a local restaurant.
Most people are happy to help when they hear of an interesting idea. Ask your friends and family to save
their drinks cans for your project, and you will soon have plenty to start you off with.

MATERIALS

◆ 4 1/2-gallon/20-litre can
◆ Empty drinks cans
◆ Enamel spray paint
◆ Large screwdriver and hammer
◆ Scissors and metal cutters
◆ Needle nose pliers
◆ Cleaning agents and damp cloth
◆ 50 rivets, 3.2mm diameter x 10.0mm head length and riveting pliers
◆ Awl
◆ Colored rope
◆ Twine or string
◆ Medium grade sandpaper
◆ Heavy-duty work gloves
◆ Large heavy-weight garbage bag

1 Wearing heavy-duty work gloves, prepare the oil can by removing the top. Use a large screwdriver and hammer to puncture a hole in the inside edge. Cut all the way around the top of the can with the metal cutters. There will be a slight lip left on the inside.

2 Lay the can down on a hard surface and hammer the lip flat.

3 Turn it upside-down and make several holes in the bottom to allow for drainage.

4 Thoroughly clean the inside of the can. Clean the outside and wipe dry. Sand the outside surface with sandpaper, removing most of the paint. Wipe clean with a dry cloth.
(see picture next column)

5 Following the manufacturer's instructions, and working in a well-ventilated area, apply the spray paint. Spray in light layers, working around the can, and allowing time for each layer to dry between coats. Leave to dry completely.

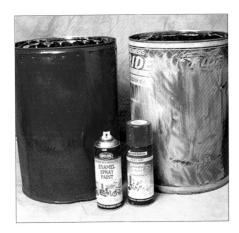

6 Measure 1in/2.5cm down from the top edge of the can and, using the awl,

punch holes every 1 1/2in/4cm all along the edge at this depth.

7 To make the flowers, cut the top off the drinks cans with the metal cutters by first cutting into the flip top hole. Cut a seam down the side and remove the bottom. Wash the cans and leave to dry.

8 Flex the cans to flatten them out. You will need about 50 flowers to cover the 20-litre can; for each flower you will need three pieces of tin of different sizes and colors. Choose the color for the bottom layer of petals and, with a pair of scissors, cut 4in/10cm squares. For the middle layer of the flower, cut 3in/7cm squares, and for the inside layer of petals cut 2in/5cm squares.

9 Cut all of the squares into circles by trimming around the edges and cutting off the corners.

10 Following close to the edge of the circle, cut a wavy edge.

11 To make the petals, cut ¾in/2cm into the inside edge of each flower, once more working all the way around the edge.

12 Use needle nose pliers to shape the petals. Grip each petal down the center and bend it in the middle by pushing one side of it down with your thumb, and bending the other side down with the pliers. Work all the way around.

13 Use the awl to make the holes in the middle of each flower. Push it carefully through the center of each layer to make a hole large enough to fit the top of the rivet through. You are now ready to apply the flowers to the outside of the tin.

14 Decide where to rivet the first flower, then take the bottom layer of petals and hold it there. Push the awl through the hole in the center and keep pushing until it punctures the can. Make the hole large enough for the top of the rivet. Remove the awl and the petal layer from the awl.

15 Take the inside layer for the first flower and push it onto the top of the rivet, then the middle layer, and finally the bottom layer. Push the top of the rivet into the hole that you just made.

16 Apply the riveting pliers to the tail of the rivet and squeeze the pliers twice to remove the tail end. Apply all of the flowers to the surface of the can in this manner.
(*see picture next column*)

17 Cut a piece of rope equal to the circumference of the top plus 3in/7cm. Bind the rope to the outside edge of the can by sewing it on with a piece of twine or string stitched through the holes.

18 Work all the way around, overlapping the two ends and binding them in tightly. Tie off the twine or string inside the can.

19 Line the inside of the can with a heavy-weight garbage bag before planting up.

aztec floor runner

The wild cats stenciled onto this *petates* represent the sun on its journey to the underworld. *Petates* is the Mexican word for a woven floor mat. It is usually made from palm or rush and is multi functional. Mats may be used in the *tianguis* (marketplace) piled high with flowers or plastic wares for sale. In the home they are used as mats for sitting and sleeping. Babies are born on *petates* and the dead are often wrapped in them for burial, just as in ancient times.

Jute twine, dyed a soft yellow, is reminiscent of the subdued color of dried corn kernels. The weaving technique used to create this rug shows a bouclé weave, which is very useful for catching dirt. Using this mat in a hallway will not do the stenciled pattern any harm. The paint is a hardwearing wood stain, which is absorbed permanently into the jute. Pre-Columbian feline creatures wind their way around the rug in an interlocking pattern.

Jute is a natural fabric that makes a very practical floor covering.

The woodwash used for the stenciling is absorbed into
the weave of the jute and will not fade even if left in the sunlight.
Try richer colors for a more exotic feel.

MATERIALS
- *Natural jute rug, 24 x 48in/60 x 120cm*
- *Woodwash for bare interior wood, green and terra-cotta*
- *Stencil card and stencil brush*
- *Craft knife and cutting mat*
- *Tracing paper and pencil*
- *Spray adhesive and newspaper*

1 Trace the template at the back of the book onto tracing paper, creating a pattern of two cats with their ears almost touching. Make three tracings.

2 Attach the tracings to the stencil card by applying spray adhesive to the back. Press into place.

3 Using a sharp craft knife, cut out the patterns on all the pattern strips.

4 Lay the floor runner out flat on a work surface protected with newspaper. Spray the backs of two of the pattern stencils with adhesive. Beginning at one short end, center the two patterns across the width of the short side, keeping the stencil close to the runner's edge and leaving a 1/2in/1.25cm border. Press the stencil into place to secure it to the jute runner.

5 Working with the terra-cotta woodwash, stir it thoroughly and dip the stenciling brush into it, soaking the end of the brush. Using a daubing motion, press the woodwash over the exposed jute runner inside the stencil. Work from one end of the design to the other (tail to ears) filling in the entire pattern of the first cat. Press the brush into the weave of the jute runner to fill in any gaps in the weave.

6 Leave the stencil in place and skip the next cat in the pattern. Press down the second stencil, this time working along the long edge of the runner. Measure the distance to be sure that the pattern will fit comfortably on the length of the runner. Press the second stencil into place with the cats' tails almost touching.

7 Paint in the next terra-cotta cat in the same way as the first. Use the third stencil to continue working the pattern along the length of the runner, keeping the edging space even.
(see picture next column)

8 When all of the terra-cotta cats are complete, wash out the stenciling brush according to the manufacture's instructions. Apply the green colorwash to the brush and paint in the green cat.

9 When all of the cats on the three stencils have been filled in, lift the stencils off the runner, laying them on newspaper. Rub the paint edges of the stencils with a rag to clean off the excess wet paint on both sides of the stencils.

10 Spray the backs of the stencils with a fresh coat of adhesive and then continue with the pattern around the edge of the floor runner, alternating colors in a regular manner. Leave to dry, following the drying time recommended by the manufacturer of the woodwash.

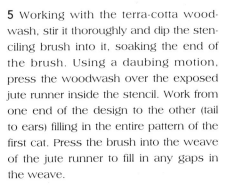

MEXICO

tin border

An unusual border can be made for a bi-colored wall with cut and pierced tin sheeting. Tin is a flexible soft metal that can be cut with scissors and punched with stamps or pierced with nails. Much of the metal work seen in Mexico is fashioned into mirror frames and candleholders; these range from the simplest frames to elaborate candelabras. Tin can be soldered or cut and folded into many folds and can be punched with leather punches made of hardened lead. This technique is worked in a similar way to stamping leather, where the stamps are punched directly onto the surface of the tin to impress images or repeat patterns. A simpler way to go about creating a pattern on tin is by piercing it with the pointed tip of a nail. By keeping the piercing closely aligned it is possible to create many intricate designs.

As the effect of punching tin forces the metal to bend with a pattern, it is difficult to keep a long strip from becoming too distorted, and so this border is made up of separate pieces. These sections can be bent inward to fit into corners, or outward to go around corners, keeping the flow of the pattern unbroken as the pattern winds around a room.

The pattern of the border shows a Spanish concho design based on a central flower with vines and leaves encircling it.

Sometimes known as roofing tin, the thin mottled metal is usually supplied in rolls
from hardware stores and building suppliers. Use professional tin snippers for cutting out the shapes,
and a spirit level for measuring height of the border.

MATERIALS
- *Roofing tin – 0.5mm tin plate galvanized steel sheet*
- *Scraps of wood ⅝in/1.5cm thick*
- *Tin cutter or scissors*
- *Panel pins or wood nails and hammer*
- *Tracing paper and pencil*
- *Spray adhesive*
- *Soft cloth and lighter fuel*

1 Enlarge the template at the back of the book. Make as many tracings of this pattern as you need to cover the width of the area to be decorated.

2 Spray the backs of the tracings with adhesive and stick the templates onto

Be sure to consider carefully the correct height for hanging the border, in accordance with any furniture that may be set against the wall and haphazardly break up the pattern.

the tin sheet. Roughly cut around the templates with tin snippers.

3 Place one piece on top of the scrap of wood. Beginning at the center of the pattern, use the hammer and a nail to punch a series of small holes along the pattern lines.

4 Keep the spacing even between each hole, and complete the design.

5 Using tin snippers, or a pair of scissors if your tin is thin enough, cut all around the punched edge of the pattern. Repeat steps 3, 4 and 5 for all your pieces of tin.

6 Carefully peel away the tracing paper from the pieces of punched tin. Clean off any adhesive residue with lighter fuel and a soft cloth.

7 Start in the corner of the room or hallway to be decorated and measure and mark the height of the pattern all along the wall. Hang the tin pieces one at a time, hammering a panel pin or nail into several holes in the pattern to hold the punched tin in place. Align the border with your measured height in a straight row.

cut paper candles

Flowers and fruit, Santos and candles, *papel picado* (cut papers) and drink, these are some of the objects to be found on altars across Mexico. Cemeteries are lit all through the night with burning candles and copal incense on Dia de los Muertos. Church altars are lined with burning *offrendas* throughout the year, lit in earnest prayer for help and guidance from the heavens. Most homes have at least a single candle offering, if not a complete altar in order to ensure good fortune for the residents.

In these cut paper candles two of the most meaningful and spiritual forms of belief have been united. Cut papers have long been used to represent spirits of the underworld, who when called upon can bring help or harm, as the caller intends. The cut paper forms might be held over smoking incense or sprinkled with alcohol and then thrown into a fire to bring the wishes of those who believe to fulfillment.

Papel picado is a magical art form where inexpensive colored tissue paper can be cut to communicate sacred and secular messages. By laminating cut paper imagery to church candles, a simple table setting can help transform an ordinary meal into one full of symbolism and magic.

These "altar" candles would look excellent grouped in different colors around a hearth.

MEXICO

By using large church candles you can gently roll down the edges over the tissue paper as the flame melts the wax within. Although there is very little risk of danger with this technique, never leave lit candles unattended.

MATERIALS

- *Tissue paper in assorted colors*
- *Cutting mat and craft knife*
- *Clear wax*
- *Large, shallow square or rectangular baking tin, 10 x 7in/26 x 18cm*
- *Church candles, 5½ x 8¾in/ 14 x 22.2cm*
- *Stapler and staples*
- *Paper punches with assorted shapes*
- *Spray adhesive and newspaper*
- *Tracing paper and pencil*

1 Place six layers of tissue together and trace a template at the back of the book onto them. Make as many tracings as you need and cut out roughly. These six layers make up one pattern.

2 Use a stapler to staple the tissue together, placing the staples in areas that will be cut away. On a cutting mat, and using a craft knife or a pair of manicure scissors, cut away the negative spaces in the pattern. Cut out the areas without staples in them first in order to

help hold the papers together. Trim around the edges and then cut out the stapled areas in the pattern last.

3 Separate the sheets of tissue. Spray the back of each lightly with adhesive. Lay the cut paper sheet on a flat surface. Apply spray adhesive to the side of the paper facing upward.

4 Lay a candle lengthwise across the edge of the design. Roll the candle along the cut paper until the two edges meet with a slight overlap.

5 With the staple in an open position, staple along the length of the seam, putting staples lengthwise along the overlapped edges. Repeat for each candle.

6 Put enough clear wax to cover the bottom of the tray. Place the tray on the top of a stove, and melt the wax over a medium heat. (Caution: Never leave hot wax unattended.)

7 Lay some old newspaper on a counter top or table surface next to the stove. One at a time, gently lay a candle in the tray of melted wax, putting the seam-side down first. Carefully holding the candle at the two ends, roll it in the melted wax. This will coat the tissue paper and secure it in place.

8 Take the candle out of the melted wax and stand it on the newspaper to harden.

9 Repeat this process for all candles, topping up the melted wax as the level goes down.

linens

▶ 81

T he projects in this chapter will enable you to introduce a Mexican flavor to every room in your home. Fabrics and needlework blend comfortably into any environment. The history of needlework from cultures all over the world is full of symbolic meaning. The weaving and embroidery of Mexico may tell the tales, whether they are true or fictitious, of a culture rich in ancient customs.

In these projects you will find deeply symbolic shamanic figures represented in neon colors in a very versatile rubber fabric, neoprene. The rough, open weave of burlap used for the brightly-colored curtain lends itself to a traditional drawn-thread pattern of a simple repeat cross pattern. Symbolic roses are embroidered

onto pillow case edges, and butterflies els are appliquéd with a stylized seashell the colors embroidered into a *huipil* of a *rebozo* (shawl), in which village the might be. The symbols of deities are protection for the wearer of the garment. woven clothing is still worn and used in occasions. We might take a lesson from and pattern permanently into our interior

onto a blanket. A set of bathroom tow-motif. In Mexican villages you can tell by (blouse) worn by women, or the weave wearer lives, or what their marital status also woven into cloth to call on divine Today, elaborately embroidered and daily life, and not just for ceremonial this idea, bringing a rich array of color design scheme.

The colors that we might associate with Mexico today are those that are created mainly with aniline (synthetic) dyes. After Mexico won its independence, trade with Europe opened up, bringing many new materials and techniques to the people. Aniline dyes were introduced, with the result that they produced brighter colors than the traditional vegetable dyes made from plants, and brought to their needlework the beautiful azure blues, hot pinks, and acid yellows that we can now use and enjoy.

The techniques used throughout this chapter call for a very basic knowledge of sewing and needlework. The butterfly blanket uses embroidery running stitches to create outlines of the characters and a few other embroidery stitches for embellishment, and the pillow cases use only a simple satin stitch throughout, which gives an exuberant density to each bloom.

LINENS

embroidered
pillow cases

Although department and linen stores have a wide range of bed sheets and pillow cases in a choice of colors and patterns, there is nothing to compare with a pillow case that has been embroidered by hand.

All across Mexico, women practice and pass on the art of embroidery, often using satin stitch only to create flower-encrusted *huipiles* (blouses). The choice of flowers, colors, and patterns used in embroidery varies from region to region. Young girls are taught the textile arts of weaving and embroidery by their mothers, who may call on divine assistance to guide their daughters' hands and their creative spirit in their work.

The extravagant full-blown roses bring an explosion of color to the plain blue pillow cases.

Embroidery threads come in a range of colors,
so you needn't keep to the colors used here; change them to suit your decoration.
Stitch the roses onto a white base and topstitch them in place.

BASIC EMBROIDERY SKILLS REQUIRED

MATERIALS
◆ *2 pillow cases, standard size*
◆ *2 pieces of white fabric the same blend as the pillow cases, 8in/20cm x 24in/60cm*
◆ *DMC embroidery thread in the following colors and quantities:*
2 skeins each #225 pale pink, #965 bright pink, #601 fuchsia pink, #718 magenta, #304 red; one skein each of #3823 pale yellow, #3822 mid yellow, #3820 golden yellow #3819 lime green, #581 leaf green, #469 moss green, and #904 dark green
◆ *Embroidery needle and hoop*
◆ *Transfer pencil and tracing paper*
◆ *Sewing kit and sewing machine (optional)*
◆ *Cardboard*
◆ *Iron*
◆ *Clear tape*

1 Photocopy and enlarge the templates at the back of the book to 4in/10cm in height. Make two copies of each and stick them together with tape. The template should now measure 18in/45cm in length. Tape the template down and secure a piece of tracing paper across the top of it. Trace the pattern with a transfer pencil. Make two copies.
(*see picture next column.*)

The flowers are embroidered with a simple satin stitch.

2 Wash and dry the fabric and pillow cases before proceeding with the embroidery. Use a few straight pins to hold the tracing paper face down on the center of the white cloth, leaving a good margin around all four sides. With a dry iron set to the correct setting for the fabric, firmly press over the tracing paper so that the pattern is transferred to the fabric. Repeat with the other piece.

3 Place the first piece of fabric to be embroidered into an embroidery hoop of a suitable size to incorporate a complete flower. Work throughout in satin stitch with three strands of embroidery thread for each color.

4 Begin by embroidering the stamen with satin stitches, which will give you a feel for this embroidery stitch.

5 Next, start on the outside edge of the flower, working around the outside edges of the petals. Then fill in the centers with the remaining two shades of pink and red.

6 Embroider the leaf with two shades of green thread, working from the outside edge in.

7 Continue down the line of four flowers and two leaves until you have completed the work. Do not tie knots; weave the ends into the stitches at the back of the work, catching up the tails under the stitches.

8 Complete both strips of embroidery and press with a warm iron to flatten out any marks left by the embroidery hoop.

9 Make a ⅝in/1.5cm hem along the long edges and iron. Place the embroidered strip across the edge of the pillow case and put a piece of cardboard inside the case to prevent pinning the two sides together. Trim and tuck under both side edges of embroidery to match the side seams of the pillow case.

10 Pin all four hemmed sides to the pillow case, matching the outside edge and side seams. Remove the piece of cardboard. Repeat the procedure on the other pillow case.

11 Sew the panel in place by hand or with a sewing machine, using thread to match the color of the cloth. Keep the stitching neat and as close to the edge as possible. Trim all the threads and press with a warm steam iron.

drawn-thread
curtain

This burnished ochre curtain is designed to give privacy, yet at the same time allow sunlight to filter through and enhance the colors. A contrasting colored backing cloth emphasizes the distinctive pattern of crosses that embellish the borders. Golden ochre is an earth mineral; its use in Mexican wall paintings dates back to ancient times.

This curtain could not be easier to make, although the idea of drawn-thread work may seem daunting. The open, loose weave of the burlap cloth facilitates the task tremendously.

By hanging the curtain with simple curtain clips, a quick solution is given to what can sometimes become a complicated business of sewing and measuring.

Drawn threadwork along the border
adds a simple but sophisticated touch to
the loose-textured curtain.

MEXICO

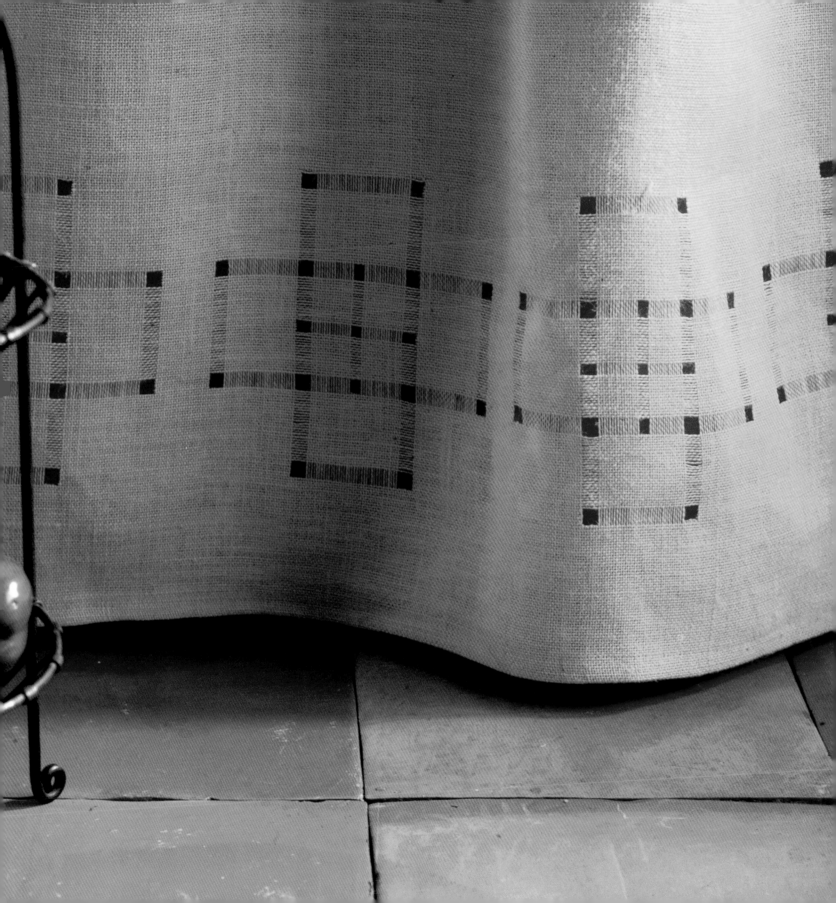

The universal symbol of a cross forms the drawn-thread design
in this easy-to-make window treatment. Choose colors to complement your room, paying
as much attention to the backing cloth as to the material for the curtain itself.

MATERIALS
- ◆ *Yellow burlap*
- ◆ *Orange cotton fabric*
- ◆ *Sewing machine and equipment*
- ◆ *Thread*
- ◆ *Manicure scissors*
- ◆ *Tweezers*
- ◆ *Pencil*
- ◆ *Ruler and measuring tape*
- ◆ *Iron*
- ◆ *Curtain clips and railing*

1 To determine how much burlap and backing cloth you will need, measure your window from the edge of the top frame to the floor, adding 4in/10cm for hems. Cut the burlap panels and cotton backing to the correct length.

2 Fold the bottom of the material over twice to make a ⅝in/1.5cm hem. Press with a hot iron. Using matching thread, stitch into place. Make a double fold at the sides of the panel to make a ¾in/2cm hem and press in place.

3 From the bottom of the hem, measure up 4in/10cm. Using a pencil, mark this depth across the width of the material and draw it in. Measure up 8in/20cm from the first line, marking and drawing it in as before.

The pattern for the drawn-thread work forms the shape of a cross along the bottom of the curtain. Use the diagram on page 109 as a guide or create your own design.

4 Starting at the side hem, and referring to the diagram on page 109, measure and mark along the two lines at the following intervals: 2⅜in/6cm, 3⅛in/8cm, then 2⅜in/6cm again. These three measurements make up the width of the first cross. Measure 1½in/4cm from the last mark to make the gap between each cross.

5 Continue to measure and mark these dimensions until you have the outside edges of four crosses evenly spaced across the width of the cloth. Draw all of these marked lines in with a pencil.

6 To complete the shape of the crosses, start at one side from the third marked line in (3⅛in/8cm). Measure and mark 2⅜in/6cm from the top line of the first set of crosses, then 3⅛in/8cm and finally 2⅜in/6cm. Go across to the fourth vertical line of this cross and measure and mark these points again.

7 You will now have the image of one complete cross. In the center square, measure and mark evenly 1½in/4cm

from the sides, top, and bottom lines. Finally, draw in the lines to form a small cross in the center.

8 Begin working the drawn-thread design by cutting horizontally across six threads in the lower left-hand corner of a cross pattern. Go up to the top of the cross and repeat in the top left-hand corner.

9 Use tweezers to help you grasp a thread and pull it out. Pull the remaining cut threads out.

10 Work across all of the horizontals in the cross, cutting the threads and then pulling them out.

11 When all of the horizontals have been pulled, work down the horizontal pattern on the cross design, cutting and pulling six threads to every line. The corners will now be open spaces.

12 Use a pair of manicure scissors to cut any ragged edges of burlap. Work across all of the crosses on the curtains in this manner.
(see picture next column)

13 Attach the backing fabric to the burlap panel. Hem the bottom as in step 1. Put the right sides of the burlap together, matching sides and hems. Allow a good 1½in/4cm overlap at the top for the curtain clips. Pin the sides and top in place and stitch the three sides.

14 Clip the top inside corners and turn the curtain right side out. Press the edges with a hot iron. Use curtain clips to hang the curtain from an iron or wooden railing.

butterfly
blanket

Not far from Mexico City, in San Juan Teotihuacán (City of the Gods) lie the great pyramids of the Sun and Moon, next to which stands the Temple of the Butterflies. There is an ancient belief that the butterfly is the spirit of dreams. What then could be a more suitable motif for decorating a blanket? A soft wool, fringed blanket, fabric dyes, and a handful of tapestry wools are all that is needed to make this beautiful project. The contrast of soft peach, over-dyed with a striking fuchsia cold water dye, forms the background for large floating butterflies.

The embroidery stitches that shape these spirits of the dream world are mainly stem, back, and daisy stitch, with an occasional blanket stitch to add interest to the patterns. Scatter these fluttering friends at random and lie back for a peaceful rest.

Larger-than life, these butterflies are the final touch to a hand-dyed blanket.

MEXICO

When purchasing the dyes, choose a dark, vivid color to go
over a paler one. Tapestry wool and uncomplicated stitches make the embroidery
work go quickly. Note that you should have the finished blanket dry cleaned.

BASIC EMBROIDERY SKILLS REQUIRED

MATERIALS
◆ *Pure wool blanket – white or off-white*
◆ *Tapestry wool – 3 skeins each of dark
peach, light peach, dark turquoise, dark
purple, light purple; one skein of dark
gray*
◆ *Size 16 tapestry needles, or needle of
a suitable size*
◆ *3 tins mandarin orange cold water
dye and dye fix*
◆ *Hand dye – deep pink*
◆ *Large plastic bucket*
◆ *Large embroidery hoop*
◆ *Dressmaker's pins and scissors*
◆ *Rubber gloves*
◆ *Dressmaker's carbon paper,
seamstress's wheel and tracing paper*
◆ *Water soluble marking pen*

Finished size: 52 x 68in/130 x 170cm.

1 Enlarge the templates at the back of
the book to the following specifications
(measurements are for the widest part
of the pattern): butterfly with circle-
patterned body 5in/12cm; butterfly
with swallowtail 8in/20cm; butterfly
profile 8in/20cm. Make tracings of
the patterns.

The butterflies are created from a variety of
stitches including chain stitch, back stitch,
lazy-daisy stitch, and French knots, in a rainbow of colored threads.

MEXICO

2 Following the manufacturer's instructions, mix up the cold water dye. (Be sure to check the weight of your blanket and use the correct amount of dye for that weight.) Dye the first color using the washing machine method. Alternatively, use a large bucket and agitate the blanket during the dyeing process.

3 Dry the blanket and mix the second color in the bucket. Top the water level up to two-thirds the bucket's depth. Fold the blanket in half across the width and accordion pleat it so that the two ends will fit into the bucket. Lower the blanket down so that the dye saturates about one-quarter of the length. It will continue to bleed up into the blanket to give a third hue. During the dyeing period, dunk the blanket in and out of the dye to help distribute the color evenly through the wool.

4 When the blanket has been dyed for the recommended time, slowly lift it out and allow it to drip back into the bucket. Wearing rubber gloves, squeeze out as

much dye as possible and hang the blanket over a outside clothesline to complete the drip-dry process.

5 Lay the blanket out on a large flat surface and place the traced patterns across the blanket, making four rows of three. Change the order of the butterflies from one row to the next.

6 Hold the patterns in place with a straight pin and use dressmaker's carbon paper and the seamstress's wheel to transfer the pattern onto the blanket. If the image is not strong enough, use a water soluble marking pen to go over the pattern.

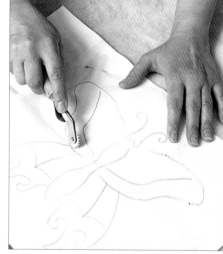

7 Use the dark gray wool and an eyelet buttonhole stitch for the circles on the body, and a stem stitch for the bodies of the other two butterflies. Complete the bodies of all of the butterflies on the blanket, keeping the loose ends on the back, and weaving them into the stitches rather than knotting them.
(*see picture next column*)

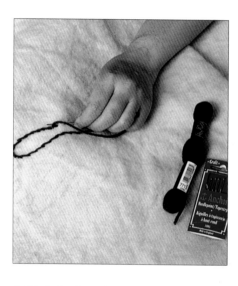

8 Stitch in the wings and their patterns using a combination of chain stitch, back stitch, lazy-daisy stitch, and french knots. Use the bright colors on the orange areas of the blanket and the light colors on the pink areas.

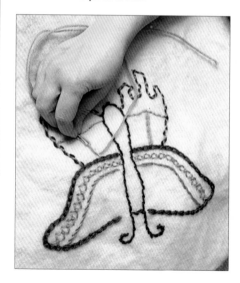

9 Tidy all the ends on the back of the blanket by weaving them in and snipping them off.

neoprene
seat cushion

It is alleged that the shamanic figures represented on this cushion will bring good luck to the owner and ward off malevolent powers. No self-respecting citizen from the village of Otomi in the Puebla region would be seen without a protective spirit to preside over their household. The spirit of the chili pepper is represented by the figure in the center of the cushion (shown in the right of the photograph), ready to lend a helping hand in the garden to ensure vigorous, heavy cropping in the vegetable plot.

The cushion can be used in the house or garden; it may be left outside in rain or shine without harmful effects. The fabric is available in a variety of colors, and it is up to you to choose whether to use the bright citrus colors shown here, or the warm, earthy, berry colors, which are more suitable for a softer natural look.

▶ 97

The hot colors used in the cushion provide a striking contrast to the cool black iron frame of the seat.

Neoprene is usually used in outdoor wear, particularly surfing and beachwear.
Its non-absorbent quality allows it to dry in minutes, making this a perfect cushion for using around a
swimming pool or hot tub. The material is available in a number of brilliant colors.

MATERIALS

♦ *2 pieces of neoprene: 45 x 50 x
¹/₈in/112 x 125cm x 2.5mm –
tangerine/citrus, 16 x 24 x ¹/₈in/40 x
60cm x 2.5mm – green*
♦ *Batting, 43 x 16in/108 x 40cm*
♦ *Cotton embroidery thread*
♦ *Size 16 embroidery needle or a
suitably sized needle*
♦ *Pinking shears and scissors*
♦ *Medium-weight card*
♦ *Glue stick*
♦ *Ballpoint pen*
♦ *Impact 2 adhesive*
♦ *Old paintbrush and newspaper*
♦ *Measuring tape*
♦ *7 strips of cardboard or paper, 14 x
1 ¹/₈in/35 x 3cm*

1 Photocopy and enlarge the templates at the back of the book so that each character is 14in/35cm tall.

2 Using a glue stick, attach the characters to pieces of card. Allow the glue to dry and cut out carefully.

3 Lay the main color on a flat surface. Mark a line 17in/43cm in from the shortest side and cut along it. Cut another piece the same size. Using pinking shears, trim around all four edges, cutting off a border of ¹/₄in/5mm, which

The characters are stuck onto the orange neoprene with bond adhesive. The sides are sewn together with running stitch.

will be the top of the cushion. Place the template of the chili pepper character on the reverse (tangerine) side of the remaining piece of neoprene. Trace around it with a pen.

4 Cut out the character carefully with sharp scissors.

5 Place the templates of the two animal characters on the reverse side of the apple green neoprene. Trace and cut them out.

6 Lay all of the characters in position on the top piece of the cushion and place a few strips of cardboard or paper around them to mark their positions.

7 Place one of the characters face down on a piece of newspaper. Follow the manufacturer's instructions for applying bonding adhesive, treating the neoprene as a porous substance, and carefully and quickly paint the adhesive onto the back of the character.

8 Touch up any areas that have begun to dry. Pick up the piece of newspaper and take it to the cushion top. Place the character down carefully in its marked position, using the strips of cardboard as a guide. Press it down firmly, then weigh it down with some heavy books.

9 Attach the other characters to the cushion cover in the same way. Leave to dry with the weights in place for up to 24 hours.

10 Using the material for the back of the cushion as a guide, cut the batting to fit the inside dimensions of the cushion. Leave a ⅝in/1.5cm border of neoprene all around the batting.

11 Lay the top piece of the cushion over the wadding and align the edges.

12 Cut a workable length of embroidery thread and thread the needle.

13 Starting at a corner, use a long running stitch to sew the two sides together. Attach new lengths of thread between the two pieces of neoprene and tuck the ends into the cushion.

14 Sew all the way around the cushion, making sure to hide the end of the knotted thread inside the seam edge.

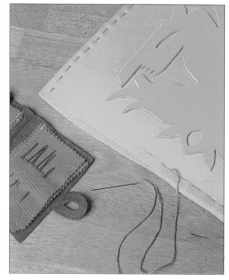

appliquéd bath towels

The image of a cross-section seashell inspired by Aztec pottery stamps makes a bold image for a set of bath towels. The shell is united with black cord appliquéd on in a wave pattern, bringing the sea and coastline of Mexico to mind. Images of water creatures are often associated with the bath; bringing these symbols into your bathroom could help to call up the spirit of water and the energies of nature.

Soft, absorbent terry cloth towels can be found in a wide range of bright Mexican colors. For best effect, mix two or three colors together. Use them to liven up a bathroom, or take them on holiday for the beach or around the swimming pool.

The black design makes a dramatic contrast to the rich colors of the bath towels.

These towels are perfect for a bathroom with a seaside theme.
Wash purchased towels before you begin the project to remove any excess
dye and allow for maximum shrinkage of the cloth.

MATERIALS
- ◆ *Terry cloth bath towels or hand towels – bright colors and black*
- ◆ *Matching thread*
- ◆ *Sewing machine and equipment*
- ◆ *Felt tip marker*
- ◆ *Round, black cotton cord*
- ◆ *Tracing paper and tape*

1 Enlarge the seashell design at the back of the book to the correct size for each size of towel. To enlarge the template to sizes more than 8 x 10in/ 20 x 25cm, photocopy the template in sections and then carefully piece it together with tape. For a bath-size towel the shell measures 13in/33cm from top to bottom, and for a hand towel, 9in/23cm.

2 Trace the shell pattern onto tracing paper with a marker. Pin in place on the black towel.

3 Cut the pattern out and remove the pins.

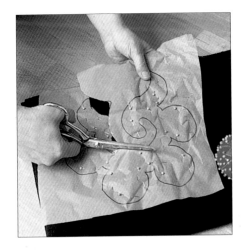

4 Place the cut-out design on the towel you are decorating, centering the design and leaving a margin of 7½in/19cm around the edges on the bath towel and 5in/12cm on the hand towel. Pin in place with straight pins.

5 Wind the bobbin with thread matching the color of the towel and loop black thread through the top of the machine.

6 Using a zig-zag stitch on a short, wide setting, sew around the edges of the shell. Trim threads and edges. Shake well to remove excess lint.

7 Take a length of black cotton cord that measures twice the width of the towel.

8 Lay the towel flat and create a wave pattern with the cord, taking it across the edging band of the towel, keeping the spacing even, and pinning it in place as you go.

9 Hand stitch the cord onto the towel. Neaten the ends at either side and trim any excess.

templates

tablecloth

actual sizes

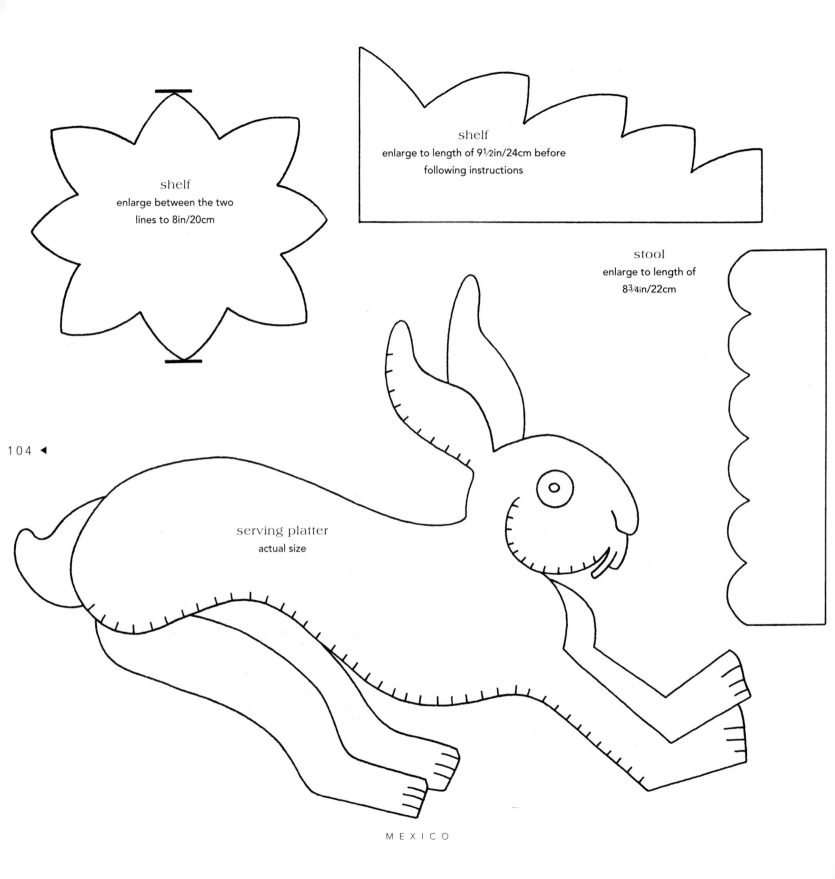

shelf
enlarge between the two
lines to 8in/20cm

shelf
enlarge to length of 9½in/24cm before
following instructions

stool
enlarge to length of
8¾in/22cm

serving platter
actual size

104 ◄

MEXICO

mosaic table

enlarge as required

cactus pots
actual sizes

file folder
enlarge as required

106 ◄

candles
enlarge to width of 8½in/21.25cm

candles

enlarge to width of 9in/ 22.5cm

pillow case
enlarge between the lines to 4in/10cm

floor runner
enlarge to height of
7¼in/18.5cm

108 ◄

tin border
enlarge between the lines to 8¾in/22cm

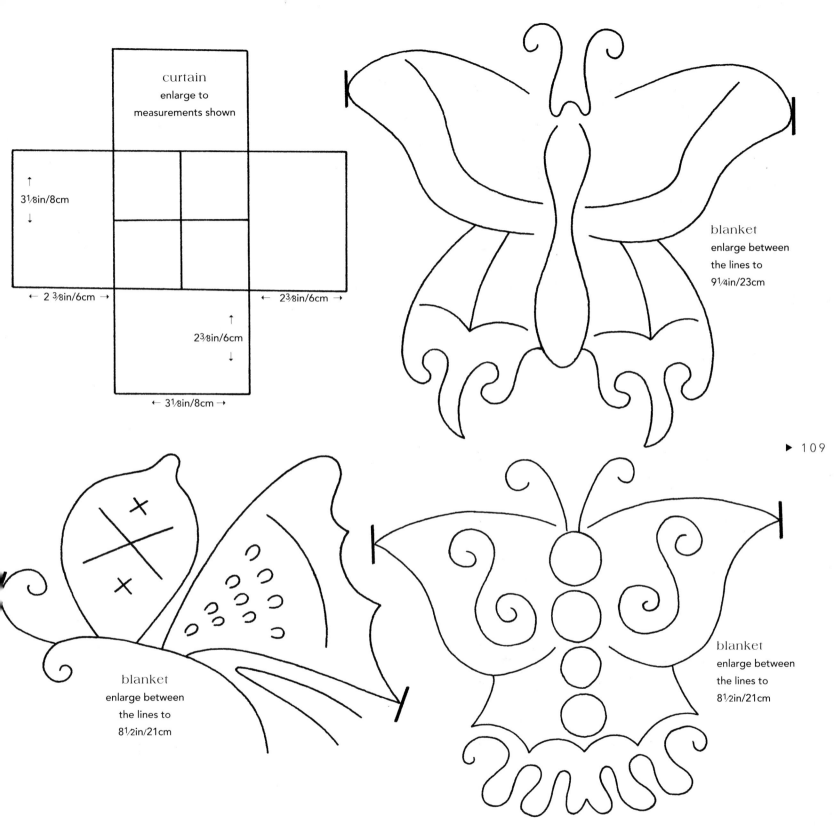

curtain
enlarge to
measurements shown

3⅛in/8cm

← 2⅜in/6cm →   ← 2⅜in/6cm →

2⅜in/6cm

← 3⅛in/8cm →

blanket
enlarge between
the lines to
9¼in/23cm

blanket
enlarge between
the lines to
8½in/21cm

blanket
enlarge between
the lines to
8½in/21cm

TEMPLATES

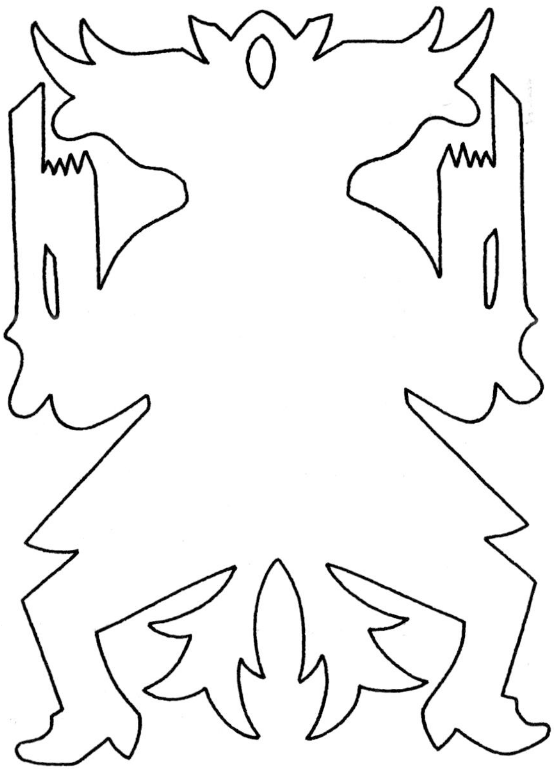

neoprene cushion
enlarge each one to height
of 14⅛in/35.5cm

You will need to
photocopy this
in two halves

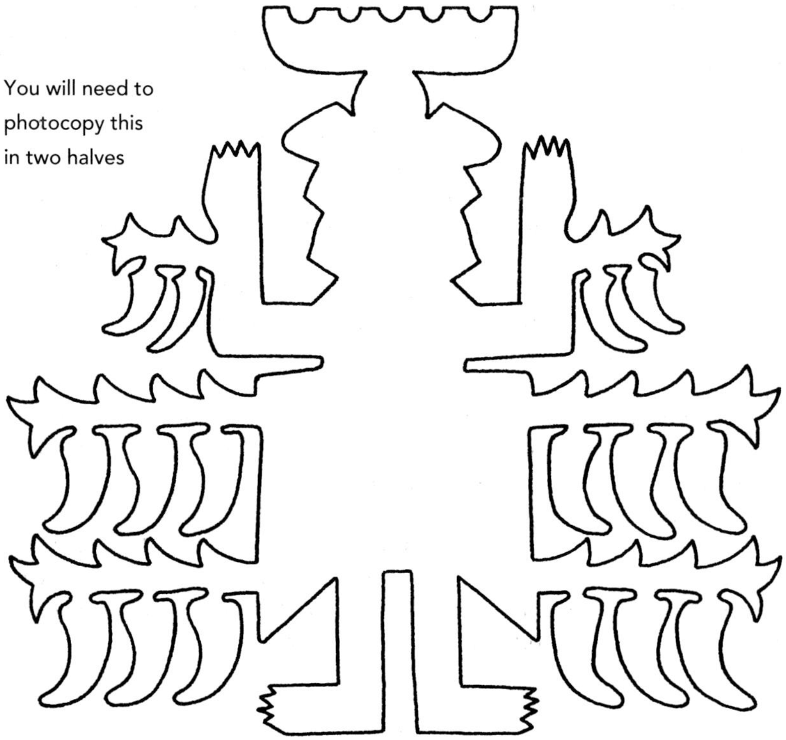

towels
enlarge as required

MEXICO

source list

MATERIALS

Colored rope, wooden file boxes & rivets available direct from Homebase Ltd, Acton, Western Circus, London W3 (call 0181 749 6982 for local stores).

Plastic lacing available from Pearce Tandy Leathercraft, Billing Park, Wellingborough Road, Northampton NN3 9BG (01604 407177).

Copper wire & metal foils available from Alec Tiranti, Sculptors Tools and Materials, 27 Warren Street, London W1 (0171 636 8565).

Raffia & burlap (hessian) available from Homecrafts Direct, PO Box 38, Haramead Road, Leicester LE1 9BU (0116 2513139).

Enamel paints and painting supplies available from Ray Munn Ltd, 861 Fulham Road, London SW6 (0171 736 9876).

Liming wax for interior woodwork available from Paintworks Decorative Paints, 5 Elgin Crescent, London W11 (0171 792 8012).

Mazurka range mosaic tiles available from Criterion Tiles, 196 Wandsworth Bridge Road, London SW6 (0171 736 9810).

Colored suede available from Pearce Tandy Leathercraft, Billing Park, Welling-borough Road, Northampton NN3 9BG (01604 407177).

Natural jute rugs and runners available from Crucial Trading Ltd, 79 Westbourne Park Road, London W2 (0171 221 9000).

Wax, wicks and candles available from Candle Makers Supplies, 28 Blythe Road, London W14 (0171 602 4031).

Embroidery & tapestry threads available from DMC Creative World, Pullman Road, Wigston, Leicester LE1 2DY (01162 811040).

Colored dyes for home and clothing contact Dylon International Ltd, London SE26 5HD, consumer advice on 0181 663 4296.

PHOTOGRAPHY

Thanks go to the following companies for supplying items used in the photography of this book:

Elephant, 230 Tottenham Court Road, London W1P 9AE (0171 637 7930) for the chair, page 16; wrought iron chair, pages 44-45; wrought iron shelf, pages 60-61; chair, page 74; table, page 77; bed, page 84; vegetable rack, pages 88-89; wrought iron bench & accessories, page 96-97.

Fired Earth Ltd, Twyford Mill, Oxford Road, Adderbury, Oxfordshire OX17 3HP (01295 812 088) for the blue glazed tiles, pages 12-13, 16; yellow glazed tiles, pages 25 & 32-33.

Jungle World at Planet Organic, 42 Westbourne Grove, London W11 (0171 221 7171) for the cacti, pages 36-37, 60-61 & 96-97; monkey trees, page 66; pineapple palm, page 74.

Emma Bernhardt, 301 Portobello Road, London W1 (0181 960 2929) for the basket, page 21; basket & flowers, page 52; flowers & sugar skulls, page 77.

Sofa Workshop, Lords Wood Barn, Lodsworth, Petworth, West Sussex GU28 9BS (01798 343 400) for the sofa, pages 36-37 & 93.

Dulux, information & stockists, 01753 550 555, for the wall paints: Dulux Trade 95BB 07/350, pages 12-13; 52, 66, 71, 96-97; Dulux Trade 83YR 44/540, pages 16, 60-61, 64, 74 & 77; Dulux Trade 74RR 28/432, pages 21, 56-57 & 101; Dulux Trade 50BG 21/328 page 25 & 41.

Graham & Green, 4 Elgin Crescent, London W11 2JA (0171 727 4594) for the lanterns, pages 41 & 77.

The Iron Bed Company, Terminus Road, Chichester, West Sussex PO19 2ZZ (01243 776 999) for the towel hooks, page 101.

index